COACHING THE

Soccer Coach Development through Functional Practices, Phase of Plays and Small Sided Games

Written By
Richard Seedhouse

Published By

Coaching The Coach 2

**Soccer Coach Development through Functional Practices,
Phase of Plays and Small Sided Games**

First Published June 2012 by SoccerTutor.com
Info@soccertutor.com / www.SoccerTutor.com
UK: 0208 1234 007 | **US:** (305) 767 4443 | **ROTW:** +44 208 1234 007

ISBN 978-0-9566752-5-5

Author
Richard Seedhouse © 2012

Edited by
Richard Seedhouse / Richard Bond / www.SoccerTutor.com

Cover Design by
Alex Macrides, Think Out Of The Box Ltd.
Email: design@thinkootb.com Tel: +44 (0) 208 144 3550

Diagrams
Diagram design by Richard Seedhouse. All the diagrams in this book have been created using SoccerTutor.com Tactics Manager Software available from **www.SoccerTutor.com**

Note: While every effort has been made to ensure the technical accuracy of the content of this book, neither the author nor publishers can accept any responsibility for any injury or loss sustained as a result of the use of this material.

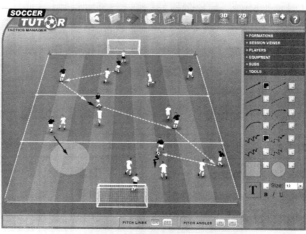

CONTENTS

Acknowledgements

This book is the third in a trilogy written as part of my personal ambition of providing affordable support for coaches involved in the development of younger players.

Joining me in my quest is George from www.SoccerTutor.com who has supported and pushed me over the last five years to complete this book. This is the second in the Coaching The Coach series and my second book published by www.SoccerTutor.com.

This book has been written for the many people who read the original book and have asked for further information on the next steps and my thoughts on coach education.

Incorporating practical sessions and discussions with many great friends and coach's it is only fair I take the opportunity to thank them now.

Thanks Barry Morris, Terry Harvey, Stuart Wilson, Paul Reynolds, Steve Ellis, Ian Weaving, Richard Steeples and Tom Stack for their influence and help over the years. Special thanks also to everyone at Coundon Court FC and Birmingham County FA especially Heidi Lockyer and Rachael Blunt.

I would also like to take this opportunity to wish my wife, Kirsten a very happy special birthday which coincides with the release of this book and thank her for putting up with me and all things Football. Thanks and I love you.

Another special mention to my mum and dad for all your support and guidance over the years!

Special thanks and appreciation has to go to Chris Morris, without whom there would be no Coundon Court FC, no journey into coaching and coach education, no coaching program and therefore no books.

This book is for Luke, believe and you can achieve!

Introduction

Firstly this book is the follow up to "Coaching The Coach: A complete guide how to coach soccer skills through drills". To get everything from this book it is strongly advised that you read that book first. In "Coaching The Coach" we concentrate on developing the coach to develop the players.

Coaching The Coach is an essential foundation in good practice and how to coach technical skills through basic drills. Coaching the Coach 2 uses this solid foundation to build coach education and knowledge through the use of coaching points, functional drills, phases of play and small sided games. This book shows us how to use our knowledge to best improve our players.

This book is also written to explain and understand the progression of drills. We look at how to progress the drills building from technical 1 v 1 drills into small sided games. We then look at how a phase of play is used and how it matches the game environment. As the chapters unfold we break them down again into individual skills and tactics to reiterate the skills and coaching points to our players before bringing it all together into a mini-soccer game.

This book does not claim to provide all the information you need or make every coach a world beater, it simply aims to be a piece of the jigsaw which fits together to educate and support coaches of young developing players, and I hope it helps you.

Key

All the diagrams follow these simple rules.

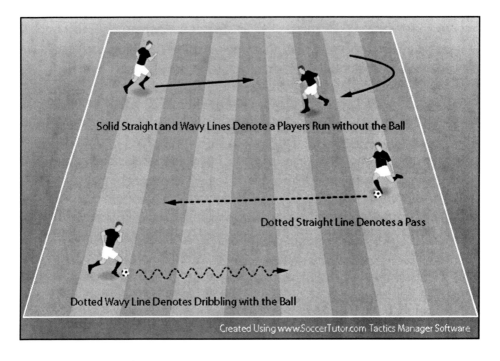

The book starts with a simple shooting drill which, by the end of the book, I trust you will never use again.

Each chapter builds on this original drill and evolves through functional drills, small sided games and phases of play with each of these progressions illustrated using one of these diagrams.

CHAPTER 1

Combination Play to Finish

SIMPLE SHOOTING - DRILL

We begin with a very simple drill. In fact I do not know a single coach who has neither seen, nor coached this drill. In the diagram below you can see our goalkeeper is ready and we have a line of players each with a ball, waiting for their turn to shoot.

The first player in line passes the ball into the coach, receives a lay off and takes their shot. The player then retrieves their ball and joins the back of the line. The next player then takes their turn.

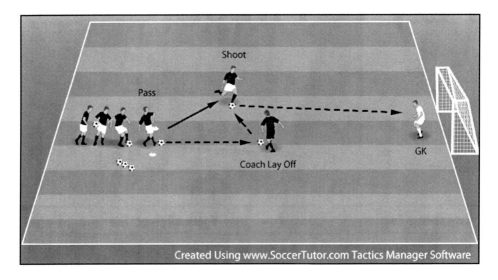

I have watched different coaches and players performing this drill many times. Almost every time we hear the coach commenting on the shot. "Unlucky", "too near the goalkeeper", "try and keep it down", "better luck next time".

Are they improving their players? No.

Are they explaining why the shot missed? No.

Are they coaching? No.

So what can we coach?

We obviously need to coach the actual technique of shooting, but how?

First, we need to understand the key points that, when performed correctly, produce a technically good shot. Only after we know these and understand how they affect the shot can we begin to coach our players.

What do you think are the key coaching points that go together to make a technically good driven shot?

1. *Approach* – The approach should be slightly from the side.
2. *Body Shape* – The standing foot is positioned next to the ball with the toes pointing towards goal, but with enough space to allow the kicking foot to swing through. The head should be steady, knee over the ball and arms out for balance.
3. *Contact* – The laces of the boot should make contact through the centre of the ball.
4. *Follow through* – A short, but sharp and strong follow-through to keep the ball down. The follow-through also needs to be in the same direction as the shot to keep the shot accurate.

Of course we always need to praise a good shot resulting in a goal or a great save from our goalkeeper. Remember this is especially important with our younger players.

Now we know these key points, we can begin to coach. Instead of commenting on what happened, we can observe and understand why it happened. We can explain the reason to our players and demonstrate how it should be done. Now we are beginning to coach.

Can you think of any problems and how we can correct them?

What if the shot goes too near the goalkeeper?

Obviously the accuracy needs to be improved. But what could be the solution? As the coach you need to watch the shooting process and assess each of the key points individually. Were they all completed correctly?

Was the standing foot next to the ball and were the toes pointing in the direction of the shot?

What kind of contact was there between foot and ball?

Was it with the laces and through the centre of the ball?

Was the follow through straight?

What if the ball went too high and over the goal? Again, it's the accuracy. So did the player contact under the centre of the ball sending it upward?

Was it the follow-through of the kicking foot, which went high when it should be low, short and sharp?

Can you spot which key point caused the problem? Yes.

Can you explain and demonstrate it to your players? Yes.

Can you coach? Yes.

How should we coach?

In what context are we using this drill?

What age group or skill level of players are we coaching?

Remember to adapt the drill and your coaching style to the players you are working with. If the session is with our younger or more inexperienced players then we should focus on one theme. To coach the shot we should concentrate purely on the technique of shooting and each of the key points that make up a good shot.

Our players will enjoy this drill as they all get the chance to score goals, but how can we make it more exciting for our younger players?

How can we add more fun?

Apart from obviously keeping score of the goals scored by each player, let's think about our younger players and their imaginations. Can we as the coach, engage with our players and paint the picture of playing for their favorite team or in a World Cup Final.

Can they score the winning goal?

Can they win the cup?

What do you think about this drill?

This drill is a good simple one for our very young or inexperienced players to practice shooting. More importantly, its simplicity allows the coach to logically run through each coaching point with their players. It also gives the goalkeeper shot-stopping practice. But can we think about the drill and try to progress it in order that we get more out of it?

Let's take a few seconds to analyze the drill.

Does the coach need to be there? No.

In a game would the coach be there? No.

Do they need to be in the middle of the drill to coach? No.

So why are they taking part in the drill?

We need to let the players play and the coach, coach.

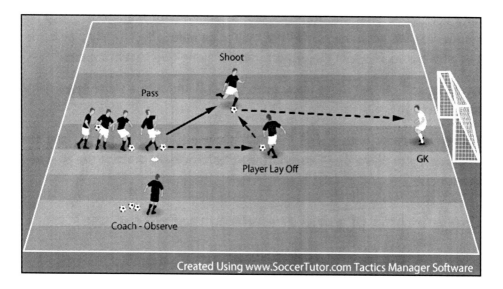

As the coach we should step back out of the drill and let our players play. We are now in a better position to observe our players, see the problems and coach our players.

So now that we have moved out from the drill, what other options do we have to coach?

We could work on our goalkeeper, their set position, shot stopping and the techniques of each particular save. But by moving the coach away what other techniques or skills have we introduced to our players?

With a player taking up our coach's position in the drill we have introduced the one-two pass. This means we can coach receiving skills, control of the ball and the weight and direction of the all-important return pass.

What do you think is so important about the weight and direction of the return pass?

The return pass needs to place the ball directly in front of the sprinting player, allowing them to cleanly stride onto the ball and dispatch their shot.

Let's take some time out from this drill to think about the one-two and the return pass. We need our players not only to be able to technically play a one-two pass but to also spot the opportunity for a one-two pass in a game.

As the coach can we move away from this drill and into a more open game environment?

Can we progress onto a drill that will allow our players to firstly see the opportunity to play a one-two, and secondly to actually practice the pass and movement?

Can you think of a drill or environment we can use?

ONE-TWO - DRILL

We will start simply by putting our players in an area, which allows free movement. We can use a 20x20 grid for 12 to 16 players. Roughly a third of the players should have a ball. The players with the ball dribble about the square looking for a passing option. The players without the ball move into space to receive a pass. Once the pass is made the original player should make a second movement to receive the return pass.

The diagram below clearly shows the passes (dotted lines) and the movement of the players (solid line).

Created Using www.SoccerTutor.com Tactics Manager Software

For younger players this is a great introduction to the one-two pass and movement. Remember to stop the drill and switch the players with the ball. This is so they all get the chance to be both the player with the ball and the player moving into space to create the passing option.

Apart from the quality of the pass what other problems might you see?

Why does one player never receive a pass?

Why does another player receive two balls from different players, even at the same time?

Communication.

The receiving players need to call the dribbling player to tell them they are free and ready to receive the pass. The dribbling players cannot just pass to any player they see. The player may already be expecting a pass from another player. They may not even be ready to receive a pass at all. Players need to communicate verbally or make eye contact and be ready at all times to receive the ball.

Congestion.

The players are getting in each other's way and bumping into each other. Players should not have their heads down looking directly at the ball. If they look a foot or so ahead of the ball they will see both the ball and the players around them.

How can we progress the drill to accommodate our older or more experienced players?

Let's think about what it's like in a game.

Is it quicker?

Is it more congested?

Is it more challenging?

Remember we need to try and create a game-speed scenario in which our players can experience seeing the opportunity, and playing a one-two pass.

Let's add the challenge of making the one-two pass and movement around another one of the players within the grid?

We have now created a free-flowing game where our players are actively looking for the opportunity to play the one-two around an opponent.

Now we need to target our coaching to the requirements of the players. With younger or more inexperienced players we may need to stop the game and show them where to play a one-two. This way we can raise their awareness of the players around them. Remember we need to get their heads up. It might even be a case of breaking down the whole technique of the pass again and logically going through the key points one by one.

Created Using www.SoccerTutor.com Tactics Manager Software

As soon as they understand the reason for the pass we can begin to let them play and see for themselves the options around them. Players learn not only from the coach but also from experiencing game situations and the solutions they create for themselves. If we want creative players we need to give them an environment, which tests them but also allows them to be creative with their own solutions.

How can we add some fun?

We can award a goal each to both players who complete a one-two around another player. Now the players are competing. Our players need to quickly spot the one-two and how, where and when to play it. They are actively looking to be involved in a one-two but are also looking to stop a one-two being played around them. Indeed they are trying to win back the ball and make their own movement and one-two pass.

We have added fun, which has increased the drill intensity and competition. More importantly we have added reality to the drill to further test our better players.

This drill could be used as part of a warm-up. It has all the game related movements at match speed and gets the players thinking.

How else might we incorporate the scoring idea into our overall session plan?

We can award an extra goal for any team playing a one-two during the free play game at the end of the training session. As the coach we need to think about our drills and how they all fit together as part of our overall session and its purpose.

Let's get back to our original shooting drill and the progressions we have seen so far. I am sure when you have seen this drill you have heard the coach telling the players to follow in their shots. Typically the player shooting follows in the shot in case of any rebound or fumbles from the goalkeeper. The passing player making the lay off stays in position and waits for the next one-two. In our original drill this player was the coach, but now we have a player in this position.

Can we think about their role and how we can add further movement making the whole drill more game realistic?

What might be a logical progression for this drill?

Is it always the player shooting who follows in the shot?

No, any player who is near the goal should close down the goalkeeper. With this in mind can we change this drill slightly and make it more game realistic?

What about the player who plays the return pass?

Let's make him more game aware, turning towards goal, reacting to the shot and following the ball into the goalkeeper. They can then retrieve the ball and go to the back of the line.

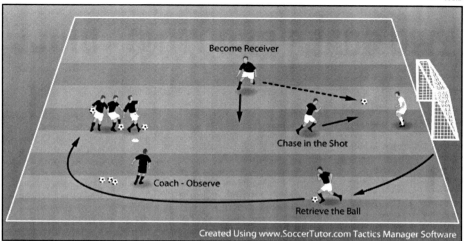

Become Receiver

Chase in the Shot

Coach - Observe

Retrieve the Ball

Created Using www.SoccerTutor.com Tactics Manager Software

The player, who shoots, immediately takes up the vacant receiving position and awaits the next players pass. The drill can then continue to rotate through the players.

Players like to score so they will get great fun out of shooting and scoring.

But how can we increase the participation and effort?

How can we progress the drill to increase speed, intensity and participation?

Could we have two drills running?

Would it be difficult to supervise two separate drills?

But do they really need to be independent drills?

Is there any way we can link them?

In the latest progression of the drill the player shooting becomes the central player and the central player chases the shot in, retrieving the ball to then join the back of the line of players.

So, let's have two goals, two lines of players and link the drills together by using one single middle player.

TWO GOALS SHOOTING - DRILL

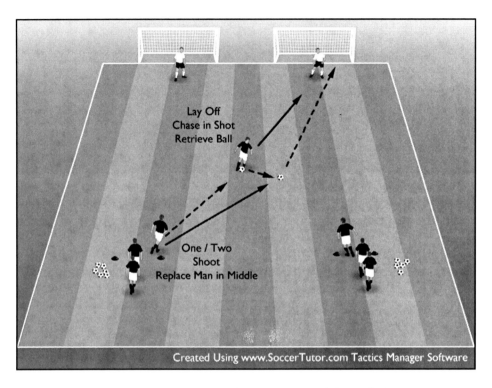

Created Using www.SoccerTutor.com Tactics Manager Software

Here we see the player at the front of the bottom-left line of players playing a one-two with the central player and taking their shot into the goal to the right.

The player shooting then takes the place of the middle player and the middle player follows in the shot, retrieves the ball and joins the line of players again.

As soon as the middle player takes their position the player at the front of the line bottom right plays a one-two with them and takes their shot into the goal top left. The drill can then continue, see diagram below.

Have we increased speed, intensity and participation? Yes.

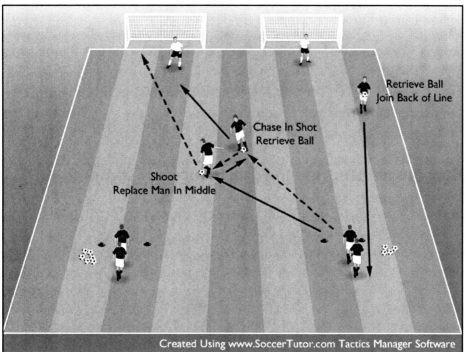

Retrieve Ball
Join Back of Line

Chase In Shot
Retrieve Ball

Shoot
Replace Man In Middle

Created Using www.SoccerTutor.com Tactics Manager Software

The play is much quicker with the players changing positions more rapidly and without the need to wait for a player to move out of the way or collect a ball as we keep swapping the goal we shoot into. This gives time for the last shot to be cleared away.

Importantly it also means the GK should always be ready for the next shot as they have time to get back up after a save or dive and prepare for the next shot without stopping the drill, which carries on into the other goal. So now we have a drill that is far quicker and allows the players to cycle through shooting more rapidly.

This is a great drill in which to coach shooting, going through the coaching points logically. This coupled with the speed of the drill adds the crucial element of challenge to the drill.

However, is there real effort or a consequence to the shot being on target or even resulting in a goal?

If we remember from the one-two drill it was competition that increased momentum, effort and fun. It was the challenge of making a one-two around another player.

So how can we introduce competition?

Scoring more goals than the other players is competitive but let's think again.

Can we use this drill another way?

Can we modify or change it to add a consequence to the shot, increasing the challenge, intensity and therefore the fun?

How can we progress the drill to increase competition?

TEAM CHALLENGE SHOOTING - DRILL

Created Using www.SoccerTutor.com Tactics Manager Software

Let's put two drills side by side and reverse one of them (as shown below). Now split all the players into two teams. The two teams can now compete against each other. How?

Each team is allocated a set amount of time to take their turn at shooting. The length of time allowed should be based on the age and fitness of the players involved.

The shooting team has players lined up at each end and a receiving player in position as if to start the two drills separately. The other team provides two goalkeepers to try and prevent goals being scored. The rest of the defending players take up positions around the goals to collect the balls of all the shots and get them back to the players of the shooting team standing in the lines as quickly as possible.

On the coaches command the players at the front of both lines simultaneously

---

start the drill by passing balls into their respective receiving players. They then receive the return pass and shoot as before. The player who takes the shot again replaces the receiving player. But this time the receiving player runs straight to the line of players on the adjacent drill. They tag the player at the front of that line allowing them to start. They then join the back of the line. This should enable the players to continue shooting, one in each drill roughly at the same time.

This drill now has competition, intensity, energy and the personal challenge for each player to get their shot right, on target and scoring a goal for their team.

Please remember even in a high tempo competitive drill like this you are still there to coach.

What are you going to coach and how?

In a competitive drill like this use the time it takes the teams to change rolls to get the coaching points across. What are they?

What are the key coaching points for a technically good driven shot?

1. *Approach* – The approach should be slightly from the side.
2. *Body Shape* – The standing foot is positioned next to the ball with the toes pointing towards goal, but with enough space to allow the kicking foot to swing through. The head should be steady, knee over the ball and arms out for balance.
3. *Contact* – The laces of the boot should make contact through the centre of the ball.
4. *Follow through* – A short, but sharp and strong follow-through to keep the ball down. The follow-through also needs to be in the same direction as the shot to keep the shot accurate.

Let's go back to our standard drill and think about another requirement for progression and adaptation.

Can we adapt the drill to replicate our team's formation and tactics?

TEAM FORMATION SHOOTING - DRILL

If our team plays mini football we might play with a single forward and have three midfielder's, one left, one right and one central. Could we use this formation within our drill?

Of course, we simply need to add the two other starting positions either side of our central midfielder. The drill now duplicates the formation of our team on the pitch. Our left and right-sided midfielders can now practice playing a one-two pass with the striker replicating a move that could be played when attacking in a game.

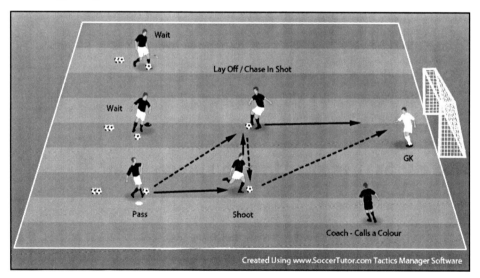

Now we have planned the organization of this new progression, how can we make the drill work?

How will it function?

Who starts the drill?

Do the players simply rotate turns?

Can we take charge of the drill as the coach, controlling the participation and momentum?

Within our drill organization we will mark each of the midfield starting positions, (right, central and left) with a different coloured cone. In the diagram above you can see we have used grey, white and black.

Now each of our players can be waiting with a ball at their feet. The drill begins when the coach shouts one of the coloured cones. The player on that cone reacts by taking their turn. Playing the one-two with the forward and shooting. In the diagram below we see the coach has shouted "black". The player on the black cone, in this case the right-sided midfielder has played the one-two with the forward and had their shot at goal.

Remember the age and skill levels of your players. This drill is now adapted to a Mini-Soccer team and its formation. The striker is turning to pressure the goalkeeper before taking their position in the free line while the midfielder is taking the strikers position. This could be a step too far for some very young players so build up slowly. Again, adapt the drill to their requirements.

So how could we vary the drill for our younger or inexperienced players?

- Each midfielder takes their shot in turn.
- Leave the striker in place while all the players take a turn.
- The midfielder follows in their shot not the striker.

Who else has benefited from this progression?

The goalkeeper. But how?

They now have to make saves from shots being taken at different angles. They also have to react and move across the goal as the coach calls the colour. This means they need to start in a central position and then use their footwork to move into line and down the line of the ball as the passes are made and the shots come in.

What else should we coach?

Let's look at the shot again. Let's think about the placement of the shot. Where should our players be shooting?

Before our players shoot what do they always need to do?

Where is the goalkeeper?

Where are they standing in relation to the goal?

Is there a large unguarded portion of the goal to aim for?

Yes.

Then shoot where the goalkeeper cannot reach to make the save. Before shooting the players must always look up and note where the goalkeeper is.

What if the goalkeeper has narrowed the angle and is well positioned.

Now where is the best place to shoot?

Shoot across the goalkeeper and into the far corner of the goal.

Why?

If the goalkeeper can only parry the ball it has a good chance of rebounding out in front of the goal for any other striker to run onto and shoot.

We have now increased and built up this simple drill alongside our improving players. A more difficult drill will only help if the players can understand and cope with its demands.

If you want to motivate your players or add fun then we again should modify our drills accordingly. In this drill our players will be enjoying themselves shooting and hopefully scoring goals anyway. But we must be careful and thoughtful, especially with the younger players.

If a player is not scoring do not let them get too far behind or singled out by their teammates. Be a considerate coach.

How?

Award a goal for a well placed pass, or the speed they chase in a rebound. Find a positive and reward it. Promote successes or endeavour in all your players and encourage at all times.

We have just spent some time looking and thinking about a very simple drill, which is used everywhere and its progressions. But can we now progress into

a small-sided game?

Why a small sided game?

Small-sided games are used to give our players more time on the ball than they would in a normal game. Small sided games can also be conditioned, enabling us to create a repetitive environment where are players can concentrate on certain skills.

If we look back at our simple drill, the one two pass, and shot, can we put this into a small-sided game?

Obviously we will need goals with goalkeepers, a striker and a midfielder or two. We also need to condition the game to make sure we repeat the pass, one-two and shot.

Have we any ideas how we can create our small sided game?

We can use a 40x20 yard area marked with marker cones for our small-sided game. We also need to add a halfway line. In this small-sided game we have the players split into two teams of four players, a goalkeeper, two defenders or players in our own half and a striker.

The rules conditioning this small-sided game are:

1. The ball must be played into the striker and the shot must be taken from within the opponents half.

2. The player making the pass into the striker is the only player able to enter the opponents half and make the option for the return pass.

3. Of course we can also let the striker shoot should the opportunity arise; they do not always have to lay off the ball.

SIMPLE SHOOTING - SMALL SIDED GAME

This small sided game will enable our players to continually try to pass, move, support and shoot.

The tempo will also be very rapid so we need to monitor how long we continue with the drill. As the coach, watch the play and if players tire use the recovery time to reiterate the coaching points we have discussed.

When we plan a basic training session we always start with a warm-up then move onto the technical drill before we finish with the game.

If we use this simple shooting drill as our technical drill can we incorporate it into a 7 a-side mini-soccer game?

This way our players can incorporate what we have coached technically into their mini-soccer game.

How can we incorporate what we have learnt into a 7 a-side end game?

We can use our small-sided game and simply increase the pitch size and zones.

This will give us a "Thirds Game" like the one we discussed in Coaching the Coach: A complete guide how to coach soccer skills through drills.

Let's look at our "Thirds Game" again.

SIMPLE SHOOTING - THIRDS GAME

This is a great Mini-Soccer drill, which promotes the formation of the team and forces our players to pass into the forwards. We will use the same formation as our previous Mini-Soccer drill. Each team has a goalkeeper, two defenders (in the defensive third) three midfielders (in the middle third) and a lone striker (in the attacking third). We can also incorporate the same conditions used in our small-sided game.

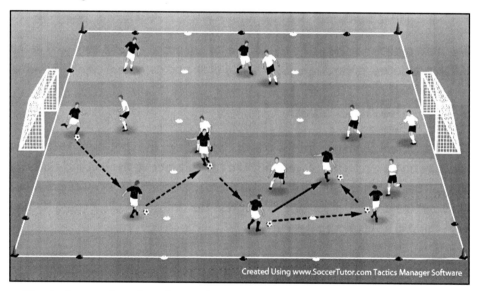

Created Using www.SoccerTutor.com Tactics Manager Software

- The ball must be played into the striker and the shot must be taken from within the opponents half.
- The midfield player making the pass into the striker is the only player able to enter the attacking third and make the option for the return pass.
- Of course we can also let the striker shoot should the opportunity arise; they do not always have to lay the ball off.

This end-game now incorporates passing and receiving, the one-two movement and the shooting we have looked at into a mini-soccer game. More importantly we have begun the thought process of really looking at the drills we read and observe from other coaches. Do they fit not only with the skill level of our players but also into what we are trying to coach?

SIMPLE SHOOTING WITH A DEFENDER - DRILL

Back to our simple drill again and let's have a think about another progression. So far we have introduced the actual coaching points of a good technical shot and progressed on to passing and receiving skills. We then added movement with our strikers closing down the goalkeeper. This means we are increasing the pressure on the goalkeeper, making it more important for them to make a clean and safe save. But what about our outfield players how much pressure has been added for them?

The main problem is this drill is too simple for our better players. Let's look at the difference between the drill and the reality of an end game and compare them.

What is the difference?

There is no real challenge for the players, apart from the shot itself. There is no pressure on the receiving player. They can casually receive the ball and easily lay the ball back. So how can we challenge them to perform under more pressure? How can we use this difference to progress the drill and make it more in-tune with the skill level of our players?

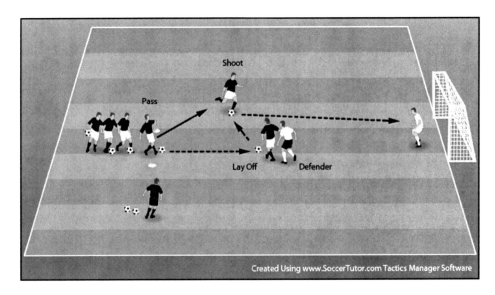

Just like the small-sided game and end game we have just seen, we can easily add pressure to the receiving player by adding a defender.

Dependant upon the quality of our receiving players our defender can be as passive or aggressive as we, the coach, deem. Let's look at the simplest form of the drill again.

What do we want to see from our receiving players?

Let's think about the game scenario and the receiving player.

We are coaching our striker to provide a one two pass, which enables our passing player to run onto and shoot. Surely, then we need our striker to be as near to the goal as possible. If the receiving player is too far away from the goal then the shooting option is not created. So our receiving player or striker should push back and hold off the defender. This in turn creates the space for our passing player to run into, receive the ball and shoot.

What do we want to see from our passing players?

The pass is actually critical to the receiving player's position.

How?

Why?

The weight of the pass! Too soft or slow and the attacker will need to come short quickly to get to the ball first. Worse still, it gives the defender the opportunity to get around the attacker to the ball.

So what makes a good pass, what were the key points that make up a good pass?

What are the coaching points for our player's to make a good pass?

1. *Approach* – slightly from the side to give enough room to make a comfortable pass. If the player moves straight onto the ball then there is a possibility of toe-poking the ball.
2. *Body shape* – the non-kicking foot should be next to the ball with the toe pointing in the direction of the intended pass. The head should be steady

and arms should be out to balance the player.

3. *Contact* – the inside of the foot should kick through the centre of the ball.

4. *Follow through* – this helps the guidance of the pass, its accuracy and the power. The follow-through should be in the direction of the pass with the force resulting in more power.

So going back to the drill we see that introducing a defender adds pressure to the player making the initial pass. It cannot be slow or inaccurate but needs to be played firmly into the receiving player's feet.

Let's go back to our receiving player and look at their technique for controlling the pass.

What would you list as the key coaching points for controlling the ball?

1. *Relax* – The receiving player should be mentally relaxed, balanced and ready, as this will promote a smooth flowing movement to receive and cushion the ball. If the player is uptight or nervous then the leg and foot will be stiffer and the ball is more likely to bounce off than be cushioned and controlled.

2. *Watch the ball* – The player should keep their head steady and their eyes focused firmly on the ball as the control is undertaken.

3. *Type of control, wedge or cushion* – The ball is either wedged between the controlling surface and the ground or the controlling surface is slightly withdrawn on impact to cushion the pace of the ball.

4. *Technique* – Does the player cushion the ball and control it correctly?

5. *Shielding* – When receiving the ball against opposition the player should control the ball away from the opponent, or keep their body between the defender and the ball.

Now we know the key points to look for and coach lets go back to the drill.

Our receiving player needs to hold off the defender while the pass is played in. They should adopt a wide barrier to stop the defender getting around them and to the ball first.

They should then control the ball as far from the defender as possible and shield the ball.

To do this they need to adopt the long barrier method and control the ball with the outside of the furthest foot whilst keeping their body between the defender and the ball.

Taking a wide side-on body stance also means they can use their arms to feel if the defender is close whilst still keeping the ball a safe distance away.

As the coach you need to watch and assess your players during the drill.

Did they hold off the defender?

Were they relaxed and able to cushion and control the ball, or did it bounce off and away?

Did they shield the ball from the defender or could the defender reach the ball to make a tackle?

Now might be a good time to look at our players and their ability to shield and keep possession of the ball. Can we think of an easy drill to help us coach the techniques and skills of shielding the ball from a defender?

What do we need to recreate this environment?

How can we do it?

What equipment do we need?

Can we prepare a simple shielding drill?

SHIELDING THE BALL - DRILL

We can use our standard 20x20 square set out with marker cones. Our squad of players is then split into pairs. The players should be matched by size and ability in order to create a fair competitive drill.

One player in each pair represents the white shirted team and the other the black shirted team. All the white shirted team's players start with a ball and they simply have to retain possession of it. Their black shirted partners try to tackle and win the ball from them.

Created Using www.SoccerTutor.com Tactics Manager Software

Can the players keep the ball within their control?

Can they shield and protect the ball?

Can they turn away from the defender?

Make sure that you repeat the drill with the black shirted team all starting with the ball and the whites trying to win the ball back.

This is a very simple drill in which we can concentrate specifically on coaching the techniques of shielding the ball. What will you say to your players?

What will you coach?

Can you list some coaching points for effective shielding and keeping possession of the ball?

1. *Observation* – The player with the ball should know where the defender is at all times either by looking or feeling.

2. *Technique* – Can the player keep their body between the ball and the defender? Keep a long barrier when the defender is close.

3. *End product* – Control the ball away from the defender. For example if the defender is to the right the player should use the outside of the left foot to manoeuvre the ball away to the left.

I am sure you can see that this drill will certainly challenge the players as they tussle to win possession of the ball. So how long can our players keep possession of the ball? If the white shirted team starts with the ball how long can they go until all of their players have lost possession?

Can we think of a way to add more competition?

As we have a black shirted and a white shirted player in each pair they can compete against each other but also as part of their teams. The competition is which player has possession of the ball when the drill is stopped. We can then count up how many white shirted and how many black shirted players have the ball. We should allow a set amount of time for the free play and then stop the drill.

As an example, if the coach stops the play as in the diagram above we see 4 black shirted players in possession and 2 white shirted players. This equates to a 4:2 win for the black shirted team. Each player who finishes with the ball should give the ball to the other player before the drill is restarted.

After breaking out to take a look at our players shielding skills and their technique of keeping possession let's go back to the original drill again. We will now take another look at the drill to see if we can make it even more game realistic? Can we think about incorporating everything we have discussed so far. The one-two, our formation, tactics all in a more game realistic environment.

FORMATION SHOOTING - SMALL SIDED GAME

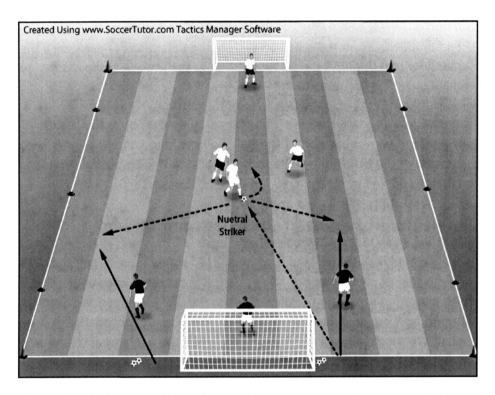

Created Using www.SoccerTutor.com Tactics Manager Software

Nuetral Striker

This small sided game will enable our players to continually attempt their one-two pass, shielding, movement, support and shooting.

The game is set up on a 30x20 pitch with goals at each end. The attacking team, shown above as black shirted, start with both players standing on the byline and a floating neutral striker in the centre of the pitch. There are two defending players and a goalkeeper. This makes a 3 v 2 overload in favour of the attacking team.

The drill starts with one of the black shirted players playing the ball into the forward and then both of them sprint onto the pitch to support the striker.

If the white shirted team gain possession of the ball they can switch their attention to attacking and try to score themselves. The neutral striker remains

with the original attacking team (black shirted in this case) until the white shirted team start the game as the attackers.

Once the game stops naturally, a goal is scored or shot goes wide the teams swap roles and the neutral attacking player also swaps to play for the other team.

For Mini-Soccer our team may play a 2, 3, 1 formation with one striker. This means the drills and games we have looked at suit our team formation and tactics. This small sided game also allows us to coach and improve our centre forwards control, shielding, receiving and passing skills. We can also coach our midfield players. Their need to support the striker quickly, provide options through attacking runs, good passes and shooting opportunities.

But let's think about our lone striker. Before the pass, control and shielding we need to work on something else.

What else do we need to coach?

Prior to being able to use our receiving skills our players need to think about getting into a position to receive the ball. If they are not in a position to receive the ball they are not affecting the game. We have talked about how to receive the ball when we are close to the defender. The striker holds the defender off using the long barrier technique. But what else could they do?

How else might our striker want to receive the ball and why?

Our striker would do well to receive the ball facing toward the opponents goal or at least half-turned so they can see the options ahead of them. This is really important in a swift counter-attack. It would also be good to get away from the defender or even receive the ball behind the defender and bearing down on the goal. So the question now is how they can get into these positions.

How can we move away from the defender to create space to receive the ball?

There are two basic moves that we can coach our players. The first move is called "Go to Show" and the second is a "Show to Go".

CHAPTER 2

Strikers Movement

STRIKER'S MOVEMENT - DRILL

Let's look at a "Go to Show". In the diagram you can see how the attacker (dark shirt) has moved away from the player with the ball; a "Go" movement. This has taken the defender (white shirt) with them. They then turn sharply and sprint back to "Show" for a pass in the space they created. The player sprints back to "show" for the pass in order to leave the defender as far away as possible.

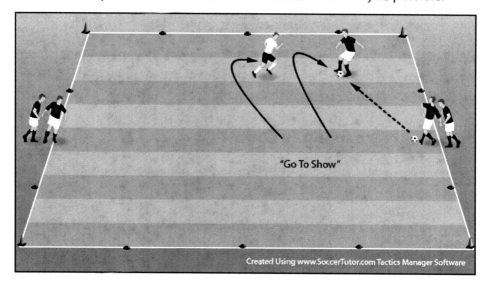

The "Show to Go" is the reverse movement, shown below.

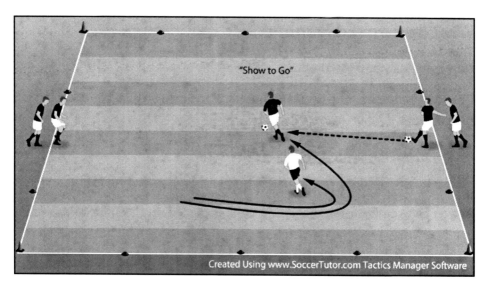

In the diagram you can see how the attacker (dark shirt) has moved toward the player with the ball for a short pass, a "Show" movement. This has brought the defender (white shirt) in close with them. They have then turned and sprinted away into the space created behind the defender, to "Go" for the long pass.

The player needs to exaggerate the movement toward the player with the ball. Why?

To make sure the defender sees the movement and goes with them so they can turn quickly and leave them stranded.

Demonstrate both of these moves to your players. Have they understood? Watch them in a drill and see how they perform. If their movement is wrong, explain the problem and demonstrate again.

So what are we trying to Coach?

The movement and receiving skills needed to get away from a marker and receive a pass.

When we coach our younger players should we coach all these receiving skills at once?

No. We need to concentrate on one technique and coach it simply and logically. So let's think of a simple drill that enables us to coach these skills.

What do we need for our drill?

How many players do we need?

One to pass the ball, one to create the space and receive it and another to pass the ball onto.

Do we need a defender?

No, we can practice the movement without a defender to begin with.

As you can see from the diagram a cone is placed on the floor to represent

the defender and we have two passing players a suitable distance away on either side of the cone. A central receiving player stands by the cone and awaits a pass.

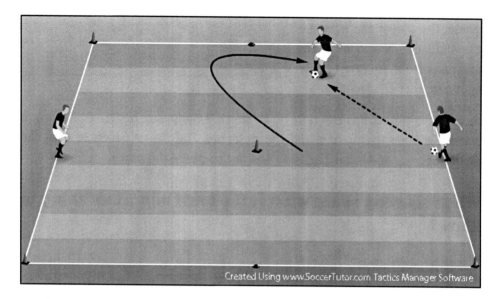

Here we see the central receiving player performing a "Go-to-Show" movement. The player sprints away before turning back to receive the ball on the half-turn, then passing it across to the server opposite. The drill can then be repeated a few times before the players change places allowing all of the participants a turn in the centre.

Could we use the same cone and players to coach a "Show-to-Go" movement?

Yes of course. Let's look at the two movements in more detail and see what impact they have on how our players should receive the ball.

Firstly the "Go-to-Show" movement.

The player making the movement should try to get far enough away from the defender to receive the pass in the half-turned position. The player should let the ball come across the front of their body in between them and the defender, trapping the ball with the inside of their furthest foot.

Why?

Created using www.SoccerTutor.com Tactics Manager Software

This will naturally open up the player's stance and their field of vision. The player can now see the defender ahead of them and can take them on or easily spot a forward pass to play.

As we have stated, this can only be achieved if the player has created enough space between themselves and the defender. The player needs to take the defender away and move back late and fast to create the space.

When creating space what is the most important thing to know?

Where is the defender?

Why is this so important?

The receiving player bases their whole decision of how to receive the ball on the defender's position relative to them. If the defender is near then they need to use the long barrier method, if they are further away then they may have the time needed to receive the ball half-turned.

How will the player know where the defender is?

When the player sprints back to show for the ball they must look over their shoulder to see if the defender has come with them and how near they are. Only then can they make a correct decision. Either the player is too near "they will have to hold them off and create the long barrier" or "yes, great movement, they can receive this pass half-turned".

Can we list the key points we have defined as receiving skills?

1. *Create space* – The receiving player's movement to create the angles and distance for the pass.

2. *Knowing where the defender is* – The receiving player needs to look over their shoulder to see where the defender is.

3. *Decision* – The player should make a decision on which type of receiving skill to use based on the defenders position.

4. *Technique* – Did the player receive the ball correctly using the appropriate long barrier or half turn technique?

5. *End product* – The player should have the ball under control and be able to play the next pass, dribble or run with the ball.

These are the points that we should be coaching our players. Coach them in a logical order with the younger players. With our more experienced players we should use them as points to watch out for and to help us with our analysis of where and why they got it wrong.

Remember, if we don't know the coaching points we will not know which point was performed incorrectly. When we know and understand them we can then explain the point, demonstrate it and see if our players have understood.

How?

Watch them perform the move again. Did they do it correctly this time?

Let's now look more closely at the opposite "Show-to-Go" movement and the way the players receive and take on the ball. In a "Show-to-Go" movement the player moves in close and drags the defender in with them to create the space beyond the defender.

The player wants the ball played into the space behind the defender so they can turn and run onto the ball. The receiving skills are now quite different. Before, we wanted close control, a steady touch, controlling the ball ready to play a pass or take on the defender.

How does our player need to receive the ball now?

We now need our player's control to be a positive first touch. We need to get the ball out of the player's feet and exploit the space behind the defender. We need to explode into the space created.

Why?

We need to sprint away and not allow the defender time to get back and make a recovery tackle.

The coaching point, end product, in our list of receiving skills for this "Show-to-Go" movement now needs to read 'exploit the space'.

We must watch our players again. Do they explode into the space they created behind the defender?

Why not?

Was the touch not positive enough?

Was it with the instep?

Could they have run through the ball using their laces to take it away or even using the outside of the foot?

Did they break their stride pattern and slow down to play the ball with their favorite foot?

Watch your players and follow the technique.

How did they perform each coaching point?

Did we see something that can be improved upon?

If there is a problem, explain which coaching point was the cause. Demonstrate the effect and the solution. Watch again and question to make sure your players understand.

So now we have looked at the strikers movements and receiving skills let's put them all together in our simple drill.

Can we use this simple drill to coach all our squad?

Would we have players standing idle watching our three players work?

How would we set out our drill to coach our squad of players?

STRIKER'S MOVEMENT SQUAD - DRILL

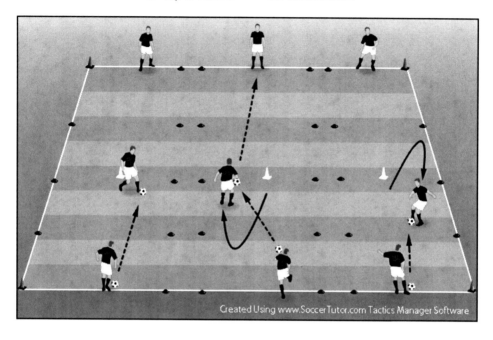

Created Using www.SoccerTutor.com Tactics Manager Software

Simple, Increase the number of drills and areas to work in.

Did you notice the channels in between the players?

When you have younger players working in simultaneous drills try and make sure you have a safety area or dead space between them. This is to make sure players are not running into each other or firing balls across other players working areas.

Let's think about this drill and our younger players.

Could they see the movement and repeat it easily?

How can we simply manipulate the drill to force our inexperienced players to make these movements, moving away and then coming short or vice versa.

How can we help our inexperienced players?

Remove the cone representing the defender and replace it with four marker cones set out in the shape of a square.

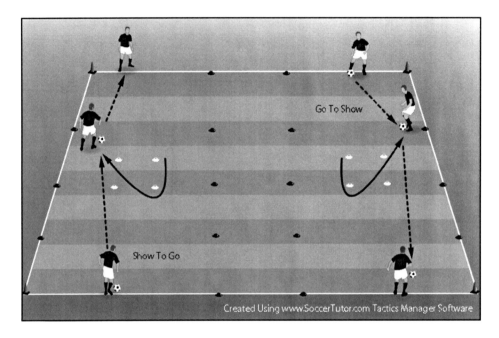

Now our players can be guided into the movement by moving around and through the cones as shown.

Let's progress this drill again now that our players know the movements they need to get into a position to receive the ball.

Can we challenge our better players?

Let's think about the last three drills we have discussed. Simple shooting with a defender, Shielding the ball and Striker's movement.

Can we add these all together and put them into a small sided game.

Can you think up a Small Sided Game?

RECEIVING AND SHOOTING - SMALL-SIDED GAME

Created Using www.SoccerTutor.com Tactics Manager Software

In this small-sided game we can see two teams of four players in a 20x20 coned square, this is set out using marker cones. Both teams have two players within the area, playing a 2 v 2 game and we have a serving player for each team on the opposite side to the goal that they are attacking. As you can see, each team also has a goalkeeper.

In this small-sided game one of the players within the square needs to receive the ball from their server on the side. The player uses the movements we have discussed to find space in which to receive the ball. They can then attack the goal either with a first time shot, if possible, or by passing to their teammates within the square to create a shooting opportunity.

During this small-sided game we need to continually rotate the players in the middle and those on the edge.

Has this incorporated all the drills?

No!

What about the original simple shooting drill we started with and the one-two?

To complete the amalgamation of all the drills we should allow our serving player to enter the small sided game creating a 3 v 2 situation within the square.

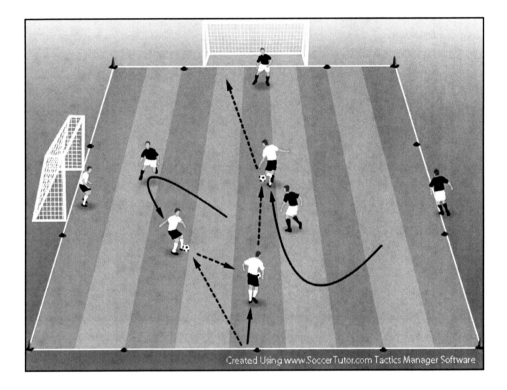

We have now progressed our simple shooting drill adding pressure from defenders. We have also included the movement of our two players trying to create space and receive the ball.

We have now created a small-sided game which allows us to coach many different techniques and skills.

But what are the key points we have defined as receiving skills?

1. *Create space* – The receiving player's movement to create the angles and distance for the pass.

2. *Knowing where the defender is* – The receiving player needs to look over their shoulder to see where the defender is.

3. *Decision* – The player should make their decision of which type of receiving skill to use based on the defenders position.

4. *Technique* – Did the player receive the ball correctly using the appropriate long barrier or half turn technique?

5. *End product* – The player should have the ball under control and be able to play the next pass, dribble or run with the ball.

What other consideration have we already seen in the book that we can add to this drill?

Team formation.

Let's consider our more experienced players again and try and use the small sided game as a basis to produce a drill more fitting them and their team formation.

We need to create a "Phase of Play"

So what is a Phase of Play?

A phase of play is a conditioned portion of a game that enables the coach to replicate the skill or technique being coached within a game scenario.

It can also be used to coach specific tactics to your team.

So what do we need to replicate in our "Phase of Play"?

Firstly we need to look at the team and its formation.

For this example we will assume that the team is playing 7 a-side, so we will play with one striker and three midfielders.

Now we want to use this phase of play to coach both the "Go to show" and "Show to go" movements.

Who should we be coaching?

We have been concentrating on our central striker's movement but in a game environment we need everyone to create space for a pass.

As we are coaching attacking play we should concentrate our efforts on the movement of the players ahead of the ball.

We also need to consider how many players we actually have in our squad. For a 7-a-side team we will assume 10 players.

How can we put it all together?

RECEIVING AND SHOOTING - PHASE OF PLAY

Created Using www.SoccerTutor.com Tactics Manager Software

Using half a pitch an attacking central defender / midfielder starts on the halfway line in possession of the ball. As in a game they have options ahead of them; players to pass the ball to. In this phase of play we have the centre forward and two wide midfielders making movements to receive the ball and we have a central midfielder supporting the centre forward. There are four defenders matching up to these four advanced players. This means we have a numerical advantage or overload (5 v 4 outfield players) in favour of the attacking team.

Is this realistic and something you might see happen during a game?

Yes, then we have our phase of play.

When do the players make their movements to receive the ball?

For younger players we can have the coach shout "Start" and the phase of play begins and everyone moves. For our more experienced players they should move as they would in the game.

This means everyone watching the player with the ball and when they lift their head prior to passing they trigger the movement. For this we need our holding midfielder or central defender to take a touch out of their feet unopposed to start the drill and trigger the movements by looking up to play the pass.

This is a great phase of play where we coach our attacking players and their attempts to create scoring opportunities.

But what about our defenders?

What do they have as a goal or challenge above and beyond stopping the attacking team?

Remember it was adding competition that increased the effort and intensity in our other drills. We need to give both the attacking team and the defending team a way to score or win.

What kind of goals or challenges could we add to the phase of play for the defending team?

If we look at the diagram below we can see a couple of extra target goals marked out with white traffic cones on each flank near the half way line. The challenge now is for the defending team to win possession of the ball and play the ball through these cones, scoring in the goals.

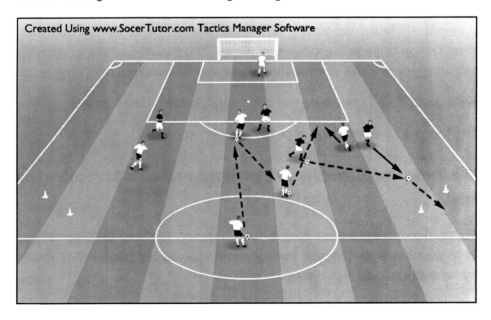

Created Using www.SocerTutor.com Tactics Manager Software

Another possible challenge could be to use an extra defending team player who operates as a target player. They would be positioned anywhere beyond the half way line and the challenge would be for the defending team to win possession of the ball and pass it into them to score.

So what do you coach in a phase of play?

The same coaching points as you coach in a drill.

So what were they?

1. *Create space* – The receiving player's movement to create the angles and distance for the pass.

2. *Knowing where the defender is* – The receiving player needs to try and keep a half turned body shape so they can see the player with the ball and the players around them. If they cannot get half turned they need to look over their shoulder to see where the defender is.

3. *Decision* – The player should make their decision of which type of receiving skill to use based on the defenders position.

4. *Technique* – Did the player receive the ball correctly using the appropriate long barrier or half turn technique?

5. *End product* – The player should have the ball under control and be able to play the next pass, dribble or run with the ball.

So what are the advantages of using a Phase of Play?

The coach can use the phase of play as an actual game environment that progresses what they have been coaching. The players will understand through actually experiencing the passage of play over and over.

Another advantage is the experience can be achieved with less players than a full game and more importantly the amount you might get at a training session.

The phase of play also allows the coach to watch the game flow carefully and see how the players perform collectively and individually.

The question is, as the coach can you spot the point in the phase of play when what you are coaching could be done by the players and if they did it correctly?

Can you stop the phase of play?

Can you question the players why you stopped the play?

Can they tell you what should of happened?

Can you demonstrate what they could of done?

We will use these phase of plays again as we continue through the progressions of our simple shooting drill. But for now let's move on again and think about another movement of our strikers.

We have looked at moving up and down the pitch to create space for a pass but what about across the pitch?

What about moving across the line of defenders.

Let's go back again to our simple shooting drill and see if we can use it to practice this new movement across the pitch and defenders.

How can we adapt the drill?

Simple, lets switch the drill around 90 degrees.

STRIKERS MOVING ACROSS THE LINE SHOOTING - DRILL

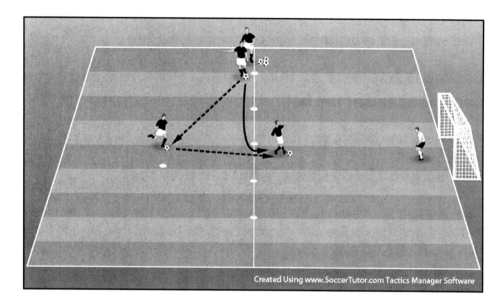

Created Using www.SoccerTutor.com Tactics Manager Software

In this drill our strikers simply line up on one end of a row of cones going across the pitch. We could use the edge of the penalty area. The first striker plays the ball into a deeper midfield player who then returns the pass in front of them and at pace so it goes beyond them and toward the goal. This enables the striker running across the pitch to turn in toward the goal and get a shot away.

This is a very simply drill that allows our players to move across the pitch, turn toward goal and shoot.

So what do we need to coach in this drill?

Let's take a closer look at the movement and more importantly the body shape of our player. Do we have any thoughts?

The player should always be in a comfortable position to see the ball and any pass but also in a position to react quickly and attack any pass played in behind the defenders.

Should their body shape change dependent upon where the ball is in relation to their run?

Let's think about a player running across the line but toward the player with the ball as in the diagram. The player can simply run face on looking diagonally to the player on their right who has received the pass and is ready to play the return. The player can see everything in front of them and toward the goal on their left.

But what happens as they continue the run and soon become ahead of the ball?

The player is now looking over their right shoulder backwards at the ball.

Is this a good body shape, what can they see?

They now only see what is behind them and away from the goal. As the player making the run gets in line with the player with the ball and then beyond them they need to change their body shape.

How?

They need to spin so they are facing forward, toward the goal, and looking over their left shoulder.

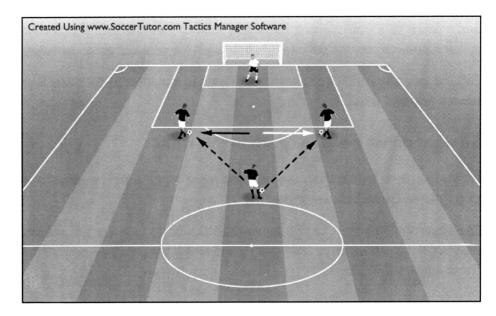

Created Using www.SoccerTutor.com Tactics Manager Software

In the diagram above we can clearly see the striker to the right of the player with the ball is facing the goal half turned and looking back over their left shoulder for the pass. The player to the left is half turned and looking over their right shoulder for the pass.

Why?

This means they can see everything around them and toward goal. They are on the front foot and ready to sprint forward as soon as the pass is played.

So now we know about this change in body shape and when it happens. As soon as the player crosses in front of the player with the ball, we need to coach it.

Can we use this drill to coach and practice this body shape change?

Of course, the second pass is simply delayed until they are past the player with the ball and have switched their body shape.

To fully understand the body shape change we need to line our players up at either end of the line of cones. This way they experience and practice both body shape changes as they move both left to right and right to left across the pitch.

Can you think of any other advantage of this body shape change?

Our striker can remain on side. Being able to see across the line of defenders means our striker can check their position and remain on side and ready to jump on any through ball.

Adopting this body shape change as they move certainly gives our striker an edge in terms of understanding the position of all the players, any potential pass and their ability to react quickly to seize upon the opportunity to shoot.

Why is an advantage for our striker to react quicker?

When this type of through ball is played the attacker is generally close to a defender and therefore space and time is limited. I am sure we can all recognize

that the quicker a shot is played the less chance the defender has of recovering.

What about the striker themselves?

Every second and third touch prior to a shot being played is also an extra chance to make a mistake, bad touch. How many times have we seen over playing in an attacking area leading to the ball running out of play, a bad touch into the keeper or a defensive clearance?

Let's promote shooting as soon as the chance arises and applaud the effort to try and score a goal.

Let's look at the coaching points for shooting again and tweak them slightly so we can coach quick shooting.

1. *Approach* – The approach should be fast and directly at the ball.
2. *Body shape* – The standing foot is positioned next to the ball with the toes pointing towards goal, but with enough space to allow the kicking foot to swing through. The head should be steady, knee over the ball and arms out for balance.
3. *Contact* – The foot nearest the ball should be used to shoot as soon as possible. The player should not break stride, manipulate the ball onto or wait for the ball to come onto their favoured foot. The laces of the boot should make contact through the centre of the ball.
4. *Follow through* – A short, but sharp and strong follow-through to keep the ball down. The follow-through also needs to be in the same direction as the shot to keep the shot accurate.

Can we encourage this movement, body shape and alertness in a small-sided game?

STRIKERS MOVING ACROSS THE LINE - SMALL-SIDED GAME

We will use our thirds game template with a simple 3 vs. 3 in the central third. In each end zone we can have a single attacker again moving along a line of cones, or the edge of the penalty area or in this case between a couple of free kick mannequins.

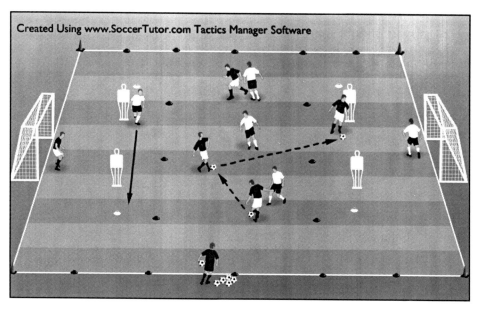

Created Using www.SoccerTutor.com Tactics Manager Software

The coach starts the drill by rolling the ball into a free player in the central area they then need to play three passes before being able to play a "killer" pass into and beyond the striker to run onto and shoot.

The strikers always needs to be alert and on the move.

Can we think of some coaching points for this drill and the movement we are trying to develop and coach?

1. *Create space* – The striker's position in relation to the ball. Can their movements along the line make sure they are always in a position to receive a through ball?

2. *Body shape* – The striker needs to be half turned ready to sprint forward at all times. They should remember if they run beyond the player with the ball to change their body shape and turn to face the goal.

3. *Awareness* – The striker needs to be on their toes anticipating a pass at any time.

4. *End product* – The striker needs to get their shot away as soon as possible.

Can we add any progressions?

- Add defenders (passive or active) to the end zone.
- Take away the cones or mannequins and see if the movement is affected.
- The players should make more passes in the middle zone before being allowed to play the pass.

Created using www.SoccerTutor.com Tactics Manager Software

If the passing is a problem for our younger or more inexperienced players then we can add a floating player. They play for the team in possession of the ball and this create a 4 vs. 3 overload in favour of them making it easier to pass the ball the required number of times.

Let's move on again and look at a phase of play introducing this new movement along with the others we have already seen.

Can we use the same phase of play we have already seen?

STRIKERS MOVEMENT
- PHASE OF PLAY

This phase of play uses half a pitch and the target goals for the defending team to attack just as before.

The attacking team line up with a centre forward, two wide players, two central supporting midfielders and an attacking central defender or holding midfielder. The defending team matches the five advanced players leaving the holding midfielder free from a defender creating a numerical advantage or overload (6 v 5 outfield players) in favour of the attacking team.

Created Using www.SoccerTutor.com Tactics Manager Software

In this diagram of our phase of play we see the centre forward and two wide midfielders making movements to receive the ball.

Our left sided player is making a "go to show" movement, our right sided player is making a "show to go" move and our centre forward is moving along the line.

We start our phase of play with our holding midfielder standing on the halfway line in possession of the ball free to make the first pass or move forward with the ball. The phase of play is then live and play continues to evolve.

As the coach we want to use this phase of play as a tool to coach the attacking player's movements to create space for a pass and shot on goal.

As discussed previously we need to watch the phase of play develop and highlight any opportunities our players have to use these new movements to get away from opponents and into space to receive the ball.

What specifically will we coach?

1. *Create space* – The receiving player's movement to create the angles and distance for the pass.
2. *Know where the defender is* – The attacking players need to know where the defenders are.
3. *Awareness* – The attacking players need to be on their toes and anticipate a pass at any time.
4. *Decision* – The player should make their decision of which type of receiving skill to use based on the defenders position, run onto the ball at pace or receive half turned.
5. *Technique* – Did the player receive the ball correctly using the appropriate long barrier or half turn technique?
6. *End product* – The player should have the ball under control and be able to play the next pass, dribble, run with the ball or shoot.

As a coach we always need to learn and develop our skills. Being able to coach a phase of play is all about understanding and seeing the game option develop and present themselves.

Can you think of an easy way to test yourself, improve and develop these skills?

How about watching a football match on the television?

Pick a theme you want to concentrate on and look for the situations that develop during the match.

For example let's concentrate on our attacking player's and the things we have learnt so far.

- Do we see a pass played into a centre forward who has to hold the ball up and shield it from a defender?
- Do we see a one-two played with an attacking player resulting in the chance to shoot?
- Do we see players going one way and then moving another to get away from a defender to create space for a pass?

More importantly do we begin to see the missed opportunities, the options and what the players could have done?

Now we as the coach are learning, developing and understanding the game.

Let's go one stage further, during the game we watched did we see any other particular ways our attacking players created space?

What about not moving, standing still?

Sounds strange but how many times did we see a ball played out to a winger standing on the touch line waiting unmarked to receive a ball. Did we see a striker or attacking midfielder just standing in between the defence and midfield or midfield and defence with no one around them.

Let's develop this idea.

We need to develop that understanding in our players, their game awareness or game intelligence.

The only way they understand is by thinking about situations, experiencing them and understanding them. We need to develop game awareness in our players. For this we cannot just coach we need to nurture an understanding.

To promote this we need to ask our players questions and listen to the answers carefully to see what they know and what they need to be told.

As an attacking player who wants to receive the ball, shoot and score, what do we need them to think about?

What should they always know?

Where am I now?

Where is the nearest defender?

Where is the goal and goalkeeper?

Is it physically possible for the player with the ball to actually pass it to me now?

How can we give our players the opportunity to understand and develop this game intelligence?

We have to coach our players in a phase of play as we have discussed. But we also need to coach them within the game environment itself.

To coach in a game we need to lay down a few rules. These have to be read and understood before attempting to coach within a mini-soccer game.

- Only coach one team during the game. This is especially true with our younger or more inexperienced players. If you think about it we also only coached one team in our phase of play.
- Question your players. Ask them where they should be, run or pass and why.
- Correct their mistakes. Only coach them if it goes wrong you cannot correct anything that leads to success.
- When coaching ask the players if they could have done something different. Lead them to the solution if they need help and demonstrate what is required.
- The coach needs to have an effective way of stopping the players in their exact positions as soon as a mistake is made. This is so the incorrect action can be shown along with the correct pass, shot or run that should have occurred. Always stop the play sharply by the use of a whistle or short command.
- At the start of the game give the players a couple of minutes of free play without coaching. Pick a reasonable time to set up the starting positions, usually after the scoring of a goal or a shot wide during the initial open play.
- Only coach the theme of your drill. Concentrate 98% of your coaching on the theme of the drill do not get side tracked by other mistakes.
- Pre prepare a set of starting positions to enable you to coach the technique or skill. For example if you are coaching dribbling the starting positions of the players should enable a pass to be played to another player who then has the opportunity to dribble the ball.

- Listen to the mood of the players; do not stop them repeatedly if it is becoming boring for them. Try to quickly put over what is required and get them to respond. The younger the players the quicker they loose interest. Do not stop the play repeatedly if it is cold or raining as the players will become cold and wet.

- Do not concentrate on running the same player over and over again. If the theme is running with the ball alternate between the players to enable them to rest using the right sided players and then the left.

- Make it as enjoyable as you can nobody learns anything while they are bored or unhappy.

- Use the planned moves to coach the ideal but watch what happens during the open play, spot the mistake and use these as an opportunity to question and improve your players.

- Do not be afraid to change the format and use your own ideas. These games are purely the starting point from which you can grow your coaching tactics and team play.

Let's use the current theme of strikers movement to develop a game in which we can develop our players game awareness.

STRIKERS MOVEMENT - MINI-SOCCER GAME

The two teams line up in their standard formations and play a normal mini-soccer game.

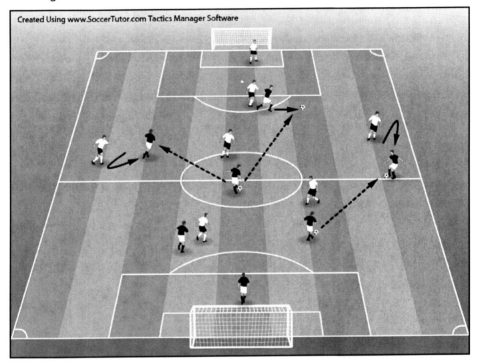

Created Using www.SoccerTutor.com Tactics Manager Software

But how de we use the game to coach our players movement, receiving skills and attacking play?

Let's look at the rules again and see if they help.

Firstly we will only coach the black shirted team as they attack.

Only coach the theme of the session.

In the diagram you can see the basic movements we want to coach.

The striker is moving across the line to receive the ball. The right sided midfielder is going away before checking back to receive the ball short and to feet, "go to

show". The left sided player is coming short for the ball before sprinting away behind the defender, "show to go".

To enable us to coach these points easily we need to prepare some simple starting positions that force the game to start a certain way.

In the diagram below we can see how the white shirted midfielder has played a forward pass which has gone straight into the hands of the opposing (black shirted) goalkeeper. The goalkeeper then throws / passes the ball to their central midfielder enabling them to pass forward again to an attacking player who has made a movement to receive it.

To add realism the two white shirted attackers have followed in the pass. Likewise the two (black shirted) defenders and holding midfielder have chased back to help defend. The white shirted midfielder playing the pass has held their position. This means the black shirted midfielder has found themselves in space for the pass from the goalkeeper by moving back toward there own goal with the play.

What do you think we can use this game and starting position to coach?

Once the ball is thrown or passed to this central midfielder we can begin to coach everything we have talked about In the previous few pages.

We can coach the attackers movement, passing, shielding, receiving, controlling and shooting.

Let's take time out before we look at coaching within this game again.

If the ball is played into the striker from the central midfielder are we comfortable in what we need to look for and coach?

Of course we are, we have seen exactly that scenario in our simple shooting drill.

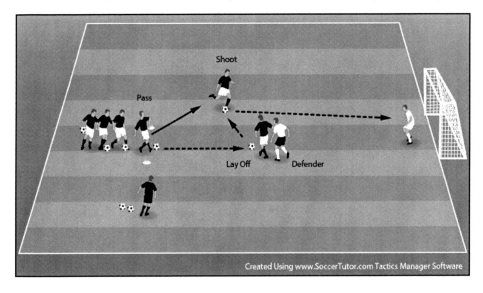

We just need to break down what we look for in the game. When we lay out our starting positions we should ask our central midfielder to play the ball into our striker. Watch for when it happens and take the same coaching points and apply them when we coach in the game.

1. *Relax* – The receiving player should be mentally relaxed, balanced and ready, as this will promote a smooth flowing movement to receive and cushion the ball. If the player is uptight or nervous then the leg and foot will be stiffer and the ball is more likely to bounce off than be cushioned and controlled.

2. *Watch the ball* – The player should keep their head steady and their eyes

focused firmly on the ball as the control is undertaken.

3. *Type of control, wedge or cushion* – The ball is either wedged between the controlling surface and the ground or the controlling surface is slightly withdrawn on impact to cushion the pace of the ball.

4. *Technique* – Does the player cushion the ball and control it correctly?

5. *Shielding* – When receiving the ball against opposition the player should control the ball away from the opponent, or keep their body between the defender and the ball.

What about when the ball goes to one of our wider players?

Of course again we know exactly what to coach as we have already listed the same coaching points for receiving the ball from our small sided game.

Created Using www.SoccerTutor.com Tactics Manager Software

1. *Create space* – The receiving player's movement to create the angles and distance for the pass.

2. *Knowing where the defender is* – The receiving player needs to look over their shoulder to see where the defender is.

3. *Decision* – The player should make their decision of which type of receiving skill to use based on the defenders position.

4. *Technique* – Did the player receive the ball correctly using the appropriate long barrier or half turn technique?

5. *End product* – The player should have the ball under control and be able to play the next pass, dribble or run with the ball.

If this is your first attempt at coaching within a game then concentrate on one scenario and one set of coaching points.

For example we may just start with the ball being played into the central forward and coaching their movement, control and receiving skills.

As we develop we may give the central midfielder the options of where and who to pass to thus giving us the chance to coach all the optional movements for all three attackers.

Please don't be frightened of coaching within this game environment.

We can build up our confidence and experience by stopping the play in the free play end game at the end of a session. As we get more comfortable we can think about coaching a theme or technique in a game.

As your knowledge and experience grows you can encompass more scenarios along the same theme. Picking out mistakes from your players, understanding them and being in a position to coach them.

As a coach you develop and educate your players but as a coach you can only do this by developing and educating yourself first.

So let's have a think!

Do you remember not moving, standing still, game awareness?

To coach it and explain it to our players we first need to understand ourselves. Do you have any thoughts on game awareness?

Let's look at our players again within our small sided game and see if we can better promote the concept.

STRIKER'S NON-MOVEMENT - MINI-SOCCER GAME

The two teams line up in their standard formations again and we play a normal mini-soccer game.

What do you think of as game awareness?

Are the players actively involved in the game?

Do they check where the ball is in relation to them, for example Is it physically possible for the player with the ball to actually pass the ball to them?

Is the attacking player aware of the game around them?

Do they know where the nearest defender?

For example can the player make a run to drag an opposing defender away to create space for another attacker?

Created Using www.SoccerTutor.com Tactics Manager Software

Or can the player stay exactly where they are which in fact is away from a defender and in a position to receive the ball?

Let's look at the mini-soccer game diagram above and look at the four attacking players.

They are all showing game awareness and understanding, but how?

Lets look what is happening and then evaluate our players.

The ball has been played by the goalkeeper into the right sided defender. The right sided defender is still quite central which means two of the white shirted players have moved toward the ball.

The right sided attacking player moves to show for the pass, a "go to show" move.

The attacking player in the centre of the pitch stays where they are as the nearest defender has moved away from them and toward the ball.

This means without actually moving they have found space in behind the defensive midfielder for them to play in.

Can you now see that the right sided defender now has options?

They could split the two white shirted players moving toward them with a decisive pass into the midfielder who without moving is now in an attacking position.

Let's see what unfolds as the ball is played out to the right hand side.

The ball is now with the right sided midfielder and the left sided defender moves toward them.

The central defender also moves over toward the defender and player with the ball to support.

This means the central forward can stand still and let the defensive players move away from them again giving them space to play in, see diagram below.

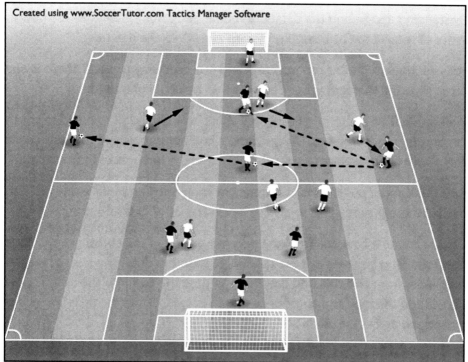

Created using www.SoccerTutor.com Tactics Manager Software

The second option for a pass is the central midfielder who is also still in a lot of space in the central area.

Let's say the ball is played into this central player. With the defenders moving across to close down the attacking right sided player the right sided defender has moved back and across to add balance to the defending team.

This however has given an opportunity to the left sided attacking player.

Let's see if our player has game awareness.

Do they check where the ball is in relation to them and Is it physically possible for the player with the ball to actually pass the ball to them?

Do they know where the nearest defender?

Can the player stay exactly where they are?

Yes.

By standing and letting the defender retreat away from them they are now in space to receive the ball, dribble forward and attack the defender.

Let's continue with the progressions and our coaching to see if there is any other situation that may arise in a game that we could of missed.

We have looked at our original simple shooting drill and progressed to coach the one, two pass and shot. The movement and non-movement to create space along with the movement across the pitch and the turn onto a through ball.

Let's think about our strikers in a game environment. Can we take one bit from each of these progressions to give us a new scenario?

Can we create a new drill from the non movement of our striker, we will have them standing centrally just like the simple shooting drill. We will also take the midfielder from this drill and use them to pass the ball into the striker. Now we will add the type and angle of pass, turn and shot from the drills where our strikers run across the pitch.

Can we put them together in a drill that allows our strikers to practice turning to receive a pass played to the side and beyond them?

Can we also test them further by creating a drill that means they do not know when the through ball is played. This should improve their reaction speed as well as their shooting.

STRIKERS TURN AND SHOOT - DRILL

Here we have the two outfield players, our midfielder and striker (with their back to goal) simply passing the ball back and forth between themselves. A goalkeeper is positioned in the full size goal behind them as shown in the diagram, left hand side.

The players continue to pass the ball until the midfielder decides to pass the ball to the side and beyond the striker, who then has to turn and shoot first time at the goal, see diagram right hand side.

This give our striker no idea when the pass is being played and keeps them on their toes.

This drill allows our striker to turn both ways to shoot first time with the left and right foot depending which side the ball is played and which is the nearest foot to the ball.

Let's quickly move on again and progress our drills. We have looked at the movement and non movement of our strikers looking to create space and receive the ball. But let's think again about its relationship to the team playing in a game.

How else might our players need to receive the ball and control it?

How does your team play?

Do they play through midfield and look for these little through balls for the strikers?

Do they ever play the longer ball?

How else might we need to control the ball?

We have used these last few drills, phase of plays and games to coach our players how to create space and receive the ball away from and close to the defender. But in all cases the passes have been short and along the ground into the striker.

Now let's look at a longer lofted pass into the strikers.

Before we can look at the new problems associated with receiving a long lofted pass we will need to look at our passing player.

They will need to have the skill and technique to perform the long lofted pass. If not we will need to coach them.

For our younger or more inexperienced players we may need to use a specific basic drill. This is so we can break down the technical points and coach them one by one in the logical order. This will give them the foundation to produce a long lofted pass.

Can you think of a simple drill that enables us to coach these key points simply?

What are the fundamental requirements we need to coach this pass?

We only need two players a distance apart and a ball.

So if we simply pair up our players, give one a ball and place them a set distance apart they should be able to practice the pass.

CHAPTER 3

Playing Through The Middle

SIMPLE LONG LOFTED PASSING - DRILL

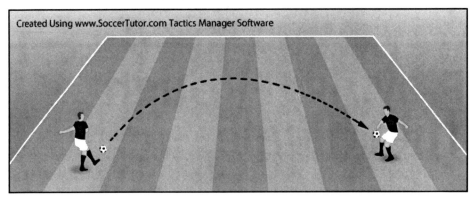

Created Using www.SoccerTutor.com Tactics Manager Software

In order to coach a long lofted pass we need to know the technical points. These should be listed logically and coached in the order that they occur.

Can you list the key points for a long lofted pass?

1. *Approach* – The player should approach the ball slightly from the side.
2. *Body shape* – The player's standing foot should be slightly back and away from the ball. This should result in the player's kicking foot slightly reaching for the ball. The head should be steady and with the players arms out to aid their balance.
3. *Contact* – The foot should make contact just under the centre of the ball. The contact on the foot should be at the top of the foot and at the base of the big toe.
4. *Follow through* – The player should have a big and high follow though to gain both height and power.

For a long lofted pass we need height and distance to go with the accuracy of the pass. Think about the coaching points for a standard side-foot pass, a shot and a long lofted pass. What are the differences?

How do you think they affect the type of pass?

Understanding the difference between these points will mean you can coach the different passes. More importantly you will be able to correct the incorrect passes.

Let's take some time to discuss them.

The approach is the same but the body shape and position in relation to the ball is different. In the case of a side-foot pass we do not want the ball to rise, it should be played along the ground. For this reason the standing foot is placed at the side of the ball and not back from the ball as in the long lofted pass. In the case of the long lofted pass the contact also changes, as again we need to loft the ball. The contact therefore has moved from the centre of the ball down and under the ball.

Finally the follow through has changed to high and powerful forcing the ball up and out toward the target player who is much further away.

It would be easy to adapt this simple drill for the side-foot pass or a driven pass (shot). We only need to change the distance between the two partner players. The important thing is to review the key technical points for the relevant pass being coached.

Can we remember the key points for a side foot pass?

1. **Approach** – Again the player should approach slightly from the side giving enough room to make a comfortable pass.
2. **Body shape** – The player's non-kicking foot should be placed next to the ball with the toe pointing in the direction of the intended pass. The head should be steady with arms out to balance the player.
3. **Contact** – The player's instep or inside of the foot should contact directly through the centre of the ball.
4. **Follow through** – The follow through depends on the distance and helps both the guidance of the pass, its accuracy and the power.

Now we can see that the actual key factors of a pass are the same and it is only the technical detail of these points that make the difference. That is to say, the way the different parts of the foot contact with different areas on the ball.

Let's tweak our simple long lofted passing drill so we can show our players the differences and maybe challenge their long lofted pass a little more.

By adding an extra couple of players we can add to the challenge.

SIMPLE LONG LOFTED PASSING 2 - DRILL

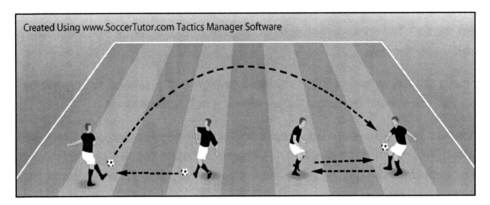

Created Using www.SoccerTutor.com Tactics Manager Software

Now the players performing the long lofted pass need to loft the ball over the middle players to their partner. The ball is then controlled, passed into the player close to them and back for their turn at a long lofted pass. This process is shown by the two players on the right hand side of the diagram above.

In this drill our players are performing short passes along the floor and the long lofted passes. Keep rotating the players so they get the chance to practice both skills.

Let's imagine we have younger or inexperienced players.

Could we go straight into a partner lofting a 40-yard pass straight over to them?

Of course not, we need to build up confidence and their ability slowly.

What would we need to change?

The distance is too far, they would not have the power to loft the ball that high and that far.

What are we actually trying to recreate in our drill?

The ball needs to arrive at the striker (our receiving player) at varying heights and speeds in order for them to practice the skill and technique of receiving and controlling the ball.

Let's think about our simple shooting drill again.

How can we modify it and progress it to enable us to coach our players to control the ball using the chest, thigh or head?

How can we modify the drill to include a long, lofted pass?

We could move our midfielder further back and have them play a lofted pass.

If we think about the game and our player's positions though, we may want our midfielder to support the strikers.

Can we include another player?

A central defender or full back could be incorporated into the drill. It would also be a good opportunity for them to practice lofted passes into our striker's head or chest.

TARGET MAN - SHADOW - DRILL

Let's adapt the simple shooting drill again by adding another player to start the drill. We will also use two strikers and two midfielders (as shown). The receiving skills, lay-off pass and shot are still a fundamental part of the drill. Now though, we can look at the long lofted pass and the striker's ability to receive and control it.

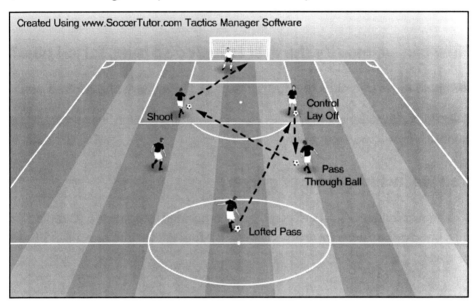

We start with our new defender playing a long lofted pass into one of the strikers. They then control the ball and play it back (lay it off) into the midfielder supporting them. The midfielder can then switch the play passing the ball into the other striker to shoot at goal.

We now have a great drill to coach the long lofted pass but what about the control and receiving skills?

For our younger or less experienced players we need a simpler drill.

Do you have any ideas for a simple drill that we can use to focus purely on coaching our players control and receiving skills?

What can we do?

SIMPLE CONTROL - DRILL

Let's make a simple 10x10 square and put some servers with a ball on each of the corners. We can then add a player working within the square. Each player working can receive and control a ball from each of the servers. After controlling the ball they can pass it back to the server. The player working can then be changed.

To begin with the servers can throw the ball into the receiving player. They can then practice controlling the ball with their head, chest or maybe their thigh.

What would be the best way to throw the ball in?

Use the drill to remind your younger players how to take a throw-in. Feet on the floor, ball over the head and release. As the players progress, the servers can move onto a looping half-volley serve.

Can you remember the key points for controlling the ball?

1. *Relax* – The receiving player should be mentally relaxed, balanced and ready. This will promote a smooth, flowing movement to receive the ball.
2. *Watch the ball* – The player should keep their head steady and their eyes focused firmly on the ball as the control is undertaken.
3. *Type of control (wedge or cushion)* – The ball is either wedged between the controlling surface and the ground or the controlling surface is withdrawn on impact to cushion the pace of the ball.
4. *Technique* – Does the player control the ball correctly?

Can you remember the fifth key point we had?

If you can it may provide a logical progression to this drill?

5. *Shielding* – When receiving the ball against opposition the player should control the ball away from the opponent.

How can we use this key point to influence how we will progress this simple drill?

If we need to coach and improve the fifth key point, which is shielding the ball, then we need to add a defender.

By adding the defender we may need to tweak the drill again.

Maybe the area will need to be a bit bigger. Maybe the receiving player should call to the server they want the ball from.

Players should continually move about within the area to find space to receive the ball. They can move away "Go" from a server and back in, "Show" to collect the ball.

To shield the ball, the player needs to receive it away from the defender. They need to keep their body in between the defender and the ball at all times.

Now we have coached the specific techniques and skills of controlling the ball and our long lofted passing.

How can we incorporate and practice these skills?

Instead of introducing our central defender or full back and elongating the drill as in our "Target Man" drill, can you think of another way of incorporating these new skills into our original simple one-two shooting drill?

LONG LOFTED SHOOTING - DRILL

Our drill is set out using half the pitch as shown. We have a player in the middle of the area to challenge the effectiveness of a long lofted pass and the rest of our squad line up on all four-corner cones.

The drill starts with one of the players on the corner cones nearest the goal.

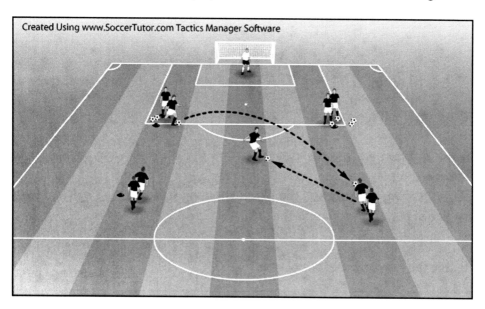

In our diagram above the player on the top left hand cone begins by playing a long lofted pass over the head of the central player to the player diagonally opposite.

They then have to control the ball using their newly acquired skills before playing a short pass into the central player.

As we see in the second diagram below, the central player then plays a return pass for them to run onto and shoot.

The players rotate after playing their passes.

In the diagram we see the player starting the drill following their pass to become the player in the middle. The player in the middle joins the line of players waiting to shoot and the player shooting retrieves their ball and joins the line of players that started the drill.

In the diagram the dotted arrows show the pass and the unbroken arrows denote the movement of the players.

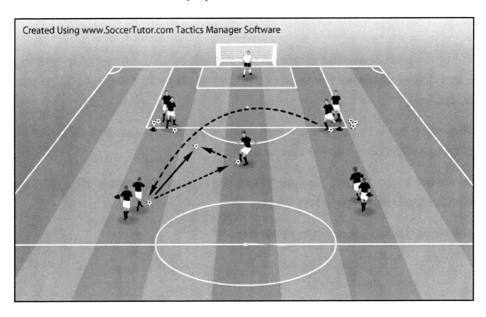

The drill then continues with the player on the top right hand cone playing the ball over the head of the central player and into the player diagonally opposite. They control the ball, play their one-two, receive the ball and shoot. The drill can then continue to rotate diagonally.

So now we have a simple but effective drill, which includes our long lofted passing, control of the ball, one-two passes and shooting.

What else might we use this drill to coach?

Remember with any shooting drill we can take the opportunity to look at our goalkeepers.

Let's take a look at their movement. Do they take small side steps keeping their feet low to the ground to move into line with the ball, narrowing the angle?

Why small low side steps?

The goalkeeper needs to keep their feet low to the ground so they are always in a position to leap and dive. If the goalkeepers feet are high they have to wait till they touch the floor again before they can dive.

Let's get back to our main drill again and our "Target Man" drill progression and run through how it works.

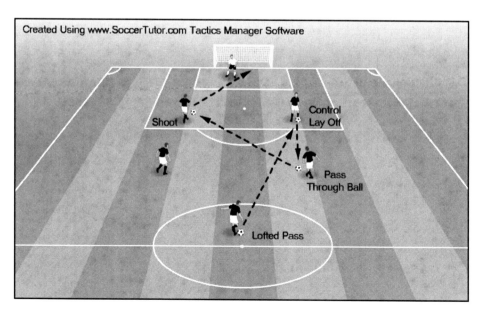

Play begins with the full back playing a long lofted pass into a striker. The striker controls the ball and lays it off to the midfielder. The midfielder then plays the ball forward into the other striker so that they can run onto the through ball and shoot at goal.

We can now use this drill to coach passing, ball control, receiving skills, shooting and shot stopping.

But how can we progress the drill again?

Obviously, when using this drill we can alternate which striker receives the pass. Maybe we can add another full back. This would allow the left back to pass into right-sided striker and the right back passing to the left sided striker. We could even add another midfielder.

Now the drill looks more game-realistic. The players are in their normal positions: centre forwards, central midfielders and defenders.

This is now a functional Practice.

- A drill that is game realistic.
- A drill that has players in the positions they would find themselves in a game.
- A drill that can be used to coach a way of playing during a game.
- A drill that coaches a tactic or way you want your players to play.

This functional practice is making our players aware of how to play through the middle of a team.

This functional practice is being used by us as the coach to show our players the tactics that we are going to use and by the players to practice these skills.

Can we add another lofted pass and test another player's control?

PLAYING THROUGH THE MIDDLE
- FUNCTIONAL PRACTICE

How about the goalkeeper?

Is there any way they could begin the functional practice?

Maybe a goal kick, throw, or drop kick to the opposing full back could start the drill.

Now we can also assess the goalkeeper's distribution and the full back's receiving skills. The full back will need to control the ball, get it out of their feet and play the long lofted pass back up to the striker.

The goalkeeper also needs to get back into their set position quickly so they are able to make any save.

How about the two strikers?

How can we challenge them?

We can add a couple of defenders just like the drill before. Again, we can make them as passive or as active as we deem appropriate. This in turn means that the midfielder receiving the ball has to make a quick decision. Does the second striker want the ball played into their feet or in behind the defence?

As the coach, we can use this functional practice to coach our long lofted passes, control, lay off and shooting. Don't get intimidated by all these different skills and coaching points. Remember, especially with the younger players, we simply need to concentrate on the theme of our session.

Let's take a closer look at the through ball as an example. This is the same scenario as the receiving drill we looked at earlier where we have a midfield player looking to play a pass into the strikers. Let's take some confidence from this as it means we simply coach the same things we coached in the drill. But can you think of anything we missed when we looked at the drill before?

What was our end product?

We did not look at taking the goalkeeper on and shooting. Let's think about our younger or more inexperienced players once more. Can we break our functional practice down and create a very simple drill which recreates what we are seeing?

It needs to enable us to coach our players to take the ball on and shoot whilst being pursued by a defender?

What are the elements that make up this part of the drill?

Do we need the long lofted pass?

No.

Do we need the other striker to lay off the ball?

No.

We only need a pass forward and three players, an attacker, defender and goalkeeper, and a goal.

SIMPLE RUNNING IN ON GOAL - DRILL

So, for this drill we will need to split our squad into pairs. The pairs should be split by ability so both partners are as equally matched as possible. The players line up against each other in two rows. The coach delivers a through ball passed in between the two players. The two players run onto the ball and compete to try and get a shot in at goal.

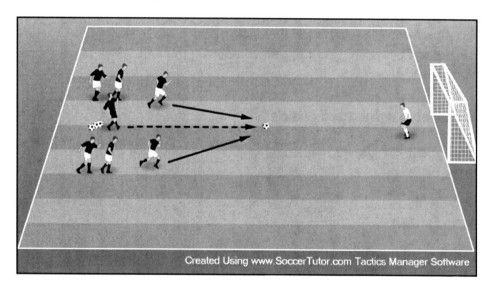

Created Using www.SoccerTutor.com Tactics Manager Software

What will we coach?

Obviously we need to coach the shot, so we will need the key factors for shooting again. Can you remember them and think about what might be different in this case?

Before, our approach was slightly from the side but do we really have time in this drill?

No.

1. **Approach** – In this case we need our players to be as fast and direct as possible. Players should be running directly at the ball and not around it.

2. *Body Shape* – The players need to be big and strong to hold off the opponent. However, they will still need their standing foot planted next to the ball with the toes pointing towards the goal when shooting. The head should be steady, knee over the ball and with arms out for balance.

3. *Contact* – Without breaking their stride pattern they should shoot with the foot that is quickest to the ball. The laces of the boot should contact through the centre of the ball.

4. *Follow-through* – A short but sharp and strong follow through to keep the ball down ensure the shot is an accurate one.

For our older or more experienced players we can talk about the mentality of a striker. A successful striker wants, more than anything, to score goals. They have an attitude or willingness to put them into a position to score above all else. We can see this by watching our players compete in this drill. Which players show the desire to score?

What else might we coach?

What about our player's movement or run once they have gained possession of the ball?

How can they make it more difficult for the other player to win back the ball or make a tackle?

Can they get their body in between the other player and the ball?

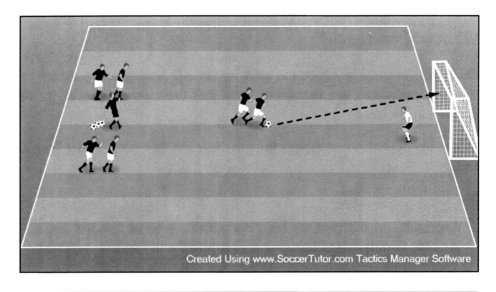

We need our player in possession to move in front of and cut across the path of their opponent.

Why?

In a game, the defender will slow, as they have to check or change stride in order that they do not foul the striker. If the defender tries to tackle and catches the striker, even by accident, then they will give away a free kick.

How can we create some fun?

We can add competition by dividing the players in the two lines into two teams. The two teams can then compete against each other to see which one scores the most goals.

What else could we do?

Let's think about the two players waiting to take their turn.

They are just waiting for the ball to be released by the coach. Let's turn them around so they have their backs to the goal. This way they will have to react to the pass, turn and sprint after the ball to shoot.

Let's change it again by making them jump, or hop, maybe they could be doing star jumps whilst waiting for the ball to be played.

This drill is now at game speed, fun and competitive. We are asking our players to compete against each other. The drill covers the skills involved in getting to the ball first and get their shot in, scoring as often as possible. We are coaching the shot by demonstrating the key points, explaining the problems we see and giving the solutions. We are now coaching our players.

Let's think again and see if this relates to what happens in a game.

Yes, of course it's representative but does the striker always find that they have a defender breathing down their neck as they close in on goal?

No.

So do they always have to shoot as quickly as possible with a first time driven shot?

No.

So what other type of shot might they use in a game?

What about a slow and accurate side foot shot, almost passing the ball past the goalkeeper and into the goal?

Thinking about our younger players, how can we adapt this drill to coach a side foot shot?

Simply remove the challenge from the other players and team. Let the player in possession of the ball dribble it as close to the goalkeeper and goal as they can before they shoot.

SIMPLE 1 v 1 SIDE FOOT SHOOTING - DRILL

Created Using www.SoccerTutor.com Tactics Manager Software

Here we have two lines of players set up a reasonable distance from the goal. You could use the penalty area if you are training on a pitch. The first player in one of the lines dribbles the ball forward toward the goalkeeper, drawing them forward before trying to side foot or place the ball into the goal. The player at the front of the other line then takes their turn and the drill continues.

Remember, if we are coaching our younger players to separate each of the coaching points and coach them one by one in the logical order. Only when they are aware of all the points can we begin to question the players about their shot and how they can improve it.

A side foot shot is in effect a simple side foot pass. So can you remember the coaching points?

What are the coaching points for passing the ball, do you understand the trigger words?

Can you explain each point to your players?

- Approach.
- Body shape.
- Contact.
- Follow through.

Let's look again at this very simple drill. Can we add anything, especially for our younger players?

We have just talked about controlling the ball. Should our attackers simply start with the ball at their feet?

No, this is not really game related.

The player would normally receive a pass or intercept a clearance. So how can we start the drill with the attacker receiving a pass?

Created Using www.SoccerTutor.com Tactics Manager Software

Can you think of any advantages if we use the goalkeeper to start the drill?

For safety reasons this is good as we know the goalkeeper is alert and ready for the drill to start and the shot that follows.

The goalkeeper could work on their distribution skills, kicking or throwing the ball out to our players.

The goalkeeper could vary the delivery to test our players' ability to control the ball.

Varying the height will mean that our players have to use different areas of their body to control the ball. This gives us the chance to continue to coach our control and receiving skills.

Can we progress this drill for our older or more experienced players again.

Let's try and add more participation and game related movements, techniques and skills.

What does our player need to do, If in a game they take a shot and it is deflected away by a defender or the keeper?

They need to react to where the ball goes and make themselves available for a second pass should they win possession of the deflected ball.

I am sure we have all seen a shot deflected back out of the penalty area and straight to the feet of an attacking midfielder.

Can we incorporate this into our drill?

DOUBLE 1 v 1 SIDE FOOT SHOOTING - DRILL

Created Using www.SoccerTutor.com Tactics Manager Software

Here, we have the same start to the drill as before. The goalkeeper throws or kicks the ball to the player at the front of the line, (top left). They dribble the ball forward and take their side foot shot.

The result of the shot does not affect the development of the drill. So, regardless of whether a goal is being scored, the shot is going wide or being deflected away by the keeper, the player shooting turns to face the players lined up (top right). See diagram above.

The first player in the line (top right) then passes the ball into the first player who returns the pass, (a one-two which they run onto), dribbles in and shoots.

The first player who shot joins the back of the line (top right) and the second player collects their ball, runs round the back of the goal and joins the line of players on the adjacent side (top left).

Now we have a more complex drill for our better or more experienced players, which has the simple side foot shot as the main coaching point.

Can you remember the coaching points?

1. *Approach* – Slightly from the side, giving enough room to make a comfortable side foot shot.
2. *Body shape* – The non-kicking foot should be next to the ball with the toe pointing in the direction of the intended shot. The head should be steady and with arms out to balance the player.
3. *Contact* – Through the centre of the ball with the side of the foot.
4. *Follow through* – this should be in the direction of the shot. The more follow through the harder the shot.

Now what else does this drill help us with?

We have spoken about game awareness and intelligence before, and this drill promotes this idea.

Just think about the movement of our first attacker after their shot and how quickly they turn to present themselves for the second attacker's one-two pass.

The first player has to switch from the shooting situation to a supporting situation very quickly. This is with the aim of capitalizing on the loose ball and the second attacking opportunity.

This transition from shooting to supporting promotes game awareness and intelligence.

Our players need to be fully aware and prepared for the fact that in football the situation changes very quickly.

Let's continue with one more drill which promotes side foot shooting and accuracy but with a lot more fun, competition and intensity.

RELAY SHOOTING - DRILL

Created using www.SoccerTutor.com Tactics Manager Software

In this drill our players are split into two teams with one team working at a time. We have two small target goals set up diagonally opposite each other and two lines of players waiting to start opposite the goals. In front of each line of players there is a ladder (cones can be used). There are then three or four balls lined up, halfway between the starting gates and target goals, ready for the players to shoot.

The other team, in this case the white shirted team, set themselves out to maintain the running of the drill. A couple of players are positioned by the goals to return the balls shot at goal and we have a couple more positioned in the middle by the row of balls. These players in the middle should maintain a good number of balls lined up ready for the working team to shoot with.

The coach then gives the working team a time limit, for example 2 minutes and the drill begins. Both players at the start of each line set off sprinting toward the ladders. They go through the ladders with two footed jumps and then emerge to run at the ball and side foot a shot into the empty target goal. They then run

to the opposite line of players and touch / tag the next player in the opposite line for them to start their turn. The drill continues. The coach should count the number of shots that result in a goal being scored.

Once the time limit is reached a score is announced and the teams swap over positions. Can the second team beat the score achieved by the first team?

This is a great drill which promotes speed, intensity and the need for accuracy in shooting.

So what can we use this drill for?

Obviously we can again coach the side foot shooting. Use the breaks in play when the teams swap to reinforce the coaching points. Don't forget to state the points in a logical order.

What about fitness?

Intense and high speed movement for a short period should be followed by a rest for the same time period. This can be repeated a number of times to help with the general fitness of your team.

Can we see any other simple progressions?

How about we allow the team not shooting put a goalkeeper in each of the goals. This will add pressure onto the attacking team.

Let's get back to our playing through the middle functional practice and our progressions.

We have looked at the runs and movement of our two central strikers and how they should control and receive the ball. We have looked at the passes into them and the type of shots.

Can we put everything we have learnt together into a final functional Practice that allows us to coach our players how to play through the middle.

PLAYING THROUGH THE MIDDLE - FUNCTIONAL PRACTICE

Created Using www.SoccerTutor.com Tactics Manager Software

As we are playing through the middle we can cut off the sides of the pitch by adding marker cones from the corners of the penalty area all the way back to the centre line. This cuts out the centre of the pitch for us to use as our playing area.

In this new functional practice we have 5 attackers playing against 2 defenders within the centre circle. We then set a rule for the attacking players. In this case they must make three passes before they can pass the ball out to one of the two central midfielders for the rest of the practice to begin.

So now we have our functional practice what are we going to coach?

1. *Create Space* – The type and timing of the run.
2. *Quality of Pass* – Accuracy and weight.
3. *Receiving skills* – Control and body shape of the receiving player.
4. *Support* – Angles and distance.
5. *End Product* – The shot.

Let's break down each point again and discuss them. Take a few minutes to think about your own comments on each point before reading on and let's see how they compare.

Creating Space

The two-midfield players should watch the passing movements within the rectangle waiting for the third pass. Once the player has received the third pass the midfielders should wait for the passing players head to rise. This is the "trigger" for the midfielder to make their run to receive the ball.

The movement of the front two strikers is critical as they only have 18 yards to work in. The furthest striker to the midfielder with the ball should move away to create space, moving to the edge of the penalty area, as shown. The nearest striker can then come straight back off the center back again on the "Trigger"

Quality of Pass

It is imperative that the pass is the correct weight. "Pass the ball don't just kick it". Use the coaching points for passing the ball to analyze and correct any mistakes. Don't forget we can always allow our players to loft the ball into the forwards, it is their decision.

Receiving and Controlling the ball

Can they receive the ball in front of them, facing forwards with an open body shape taking the ball on the back foot. Are they relaxed and comfortable controlling the ball with one touch ready for the next pass.

Support

The other midfielder should come across deep and central to support, as shown. This is primarily to provide passing options if the ball goes to the retreating striker, a one-two for example, but secondly to allow them to burst through the central gap left by the two forwards.

End Product

The final shot on goal is the end product and in all cases should be accurate and technically correct.

In all cases we as the coach need to know the coaching points for each of these specific areas in order to coach them.

As the whole point of a game of football is to score more goals than your opponents let's see what you will coach when we come to the end product.

What are the coaching points for shooting?

1. *Approach* – The players should approach the ball slightly from the side, time allowing, or sprint onto the ball and shoot.
2. *Body Shape* – The players need their standing foot planted next to the ball with the toes pointing towards the goal when shooting. The head should be steady, knee over the ball and with arms out for balance.
3. *Contact* – The laces of the boot should contact through the centre of the ball for a longer range shot or the inside of the foot for a close range pass type shot.
4. *Follow-through* – A short but sharp and strong follow through to keep the ball down ensure the shot is an accurate one.

Can we progress this functional practice?

Add a defending midfielder.

This will add pressure onto the initial pass, as when the third pass is played the player needs to look up and see where the defending midfielder is. It will also add pressure onto the player receiving the ball as, just like in a game, they will have less time to make their decision and pass.

So where do we go next?

What about playing the ball out to our wide midfielders or wingers?

Let's try and incorporate them into our original target man functional practice.

CHAPTER 4

Playing Out Wide

PLAYING OUT WIDE - FUNCTIONAL PRACTICE

Firstly do we remember what a functional practice is?

A drill that is game-realistic, having the players in the positions they would find themselves in a game.

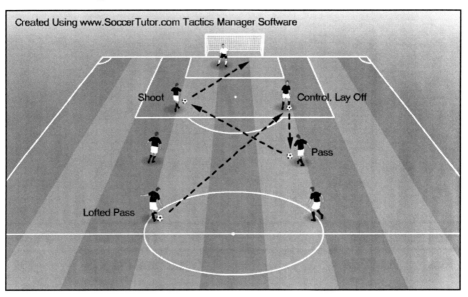

Created Using www.SoccerTutor.com Tactics Manager Software

Shoot

Control, Lay Off

Pass

Lofted Pass

Let's take another look at this drill. We have two strikers and the midfielder playing the through ball.

Does the midfielder have to play the ball to the strikers?

In this drill and more importantly in a game, would there be more options and where could they be?

In this drill we can see the other central midfielder who could show for a pass. In the game environment there may be a wider player or winger available. Let's add these wide players into the drill and see what options and ideas we have.

As before, the drill starts with a long lofted pass, played into our centre forward who in turn lays the ball back to the midfield player.

Now what can we do?

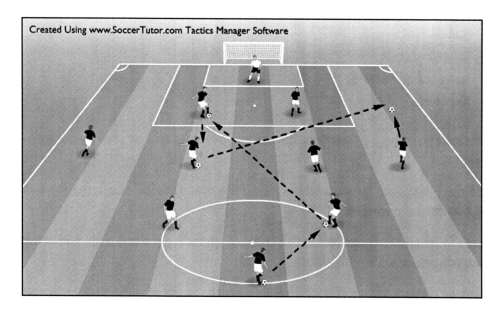

Created Using www.SoccerTutor.com Tactics Manager Software

I think we can all see the new options. By laying out the team's formation we see the ball can be played straight out to the wing for our wide player to run onto.

Now instead of attacking through the middle we are looking at attacking by going wide. This involves getting the ball to our wingers and allowing them to cross the ball for our strikers to try and score.

To keep everyone involved in this drill we still need to vary the passes and which wing the ball goes out to.

In the diagram above the right-sided defender hits a long diagonal ball to the left-sided forward. They lay the ball straight back for the central midfielder to hit a long diagonal ball to the right-sided winger.

This can be alternated with the left-sided defender hitting a diagonal ball to the right-sided forward, whose lay off can then be played to the left winger to cross.

This pattern of play is easily dictated by which player the central defender passes to when starting the drill

What can we coach within this functional practice?

- Ball control.
- Receiving skills.
- Long Lofted Passing.
- Shooting.

We are also using our functional practice to promote a tactic used by our team in games.

All the players are seeing and practicing the coach's tactic of playing the ball out wide to the wingers.

Let's focus and concentrate on this tactic of spreading the ball wide and using our wingers or wide midfielders.

Can we prepare a basic drill which will promote the use of width to our players?

Can we make the players go wide?

Can you think of a drill that promotes width?

THREE GOALS GAME
- SMALL SIDED GAME

Let's manipulate and add rules to another 4 v 4 small sided game.

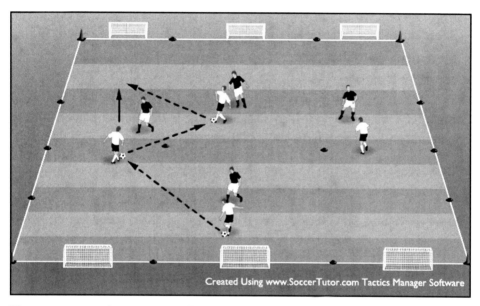

Created Using www.SoccerTutor.com Tactics Manager Software

Three target goals are set up along two opposite sides of our playing area and a halfway line is added, purely as a marker. Our two teams of four players then play a normal game within the area with the objective of scoring a goal in one of opposite three goals.

To force the teams to think about playing wide we have the three target goals.

Can we do more?

We will also have a skewed scoring system. A goal scored in the central goals scores one goal as normal. A goal scored in either of the wide goals counts double.

Now we have a free flowing small sided game which promotes the use of the full width of the pitch to our players.

Can you think about this small sided game and what skills we have looked at?

Can we highlight any of them to our players during the game?

All the skills we have talked about can be incorporated.

- Receiving skills, half turned and wide barrier.
- Control
- One-Two passing
- Shooting, driven and side foot shooting.
- Movement, go to show, show to go and movement across the line.
- Long lofted passing

Remember if we are using this small sided game with younger players stick to one theme and only coach the topic of the session.

With older players we can let them play and maybe target our coaching more to the individual player and their developmental requirements.

Can we move on again quickly using the same small sided game format.

Let's think about the progression. We now have the players looking wide and playing the ball wide. But in this drill that was the end of the challenge as the next step was a shot at goal.

Is this realistic for our older players or would we want more?

Can we now take away the three goals and make the small sided game more game related by just using the single central goal.

Hopefully now we will have our wide players receiving the ball moving down the wing and crossing the ball.

Can we force this again?

Another rule.

Our players can only score from a cross.

CROSSING GAME - SMALL SIDED GAME

Created Using www.SoccerTutor.com Tactics Manager Software

Here we have another 4 v 4 small sided game, this time with a single full size goal at each end of the 40x30 playing area. Our players are told they can only score from a cross. This means the players spread out to allow the ball to be passed out wide for the cross to come over.

In the diagram above we see the ball played into our target striker who lays the ball off out wide. They then turn and spin into the near post while our opposite wide player moves infield toward goal to support.

This is great movement from our players and maybe something we want to coach as a tactic for our games. Maybe we want to work with two strikers and the way they attack a cross as a pair.

A small sided game is not really the place to continually coach a tactic like this.

How can we coach this movement as a desired tactic for our players?

How about using a functional practice?

SIMPLE CROSSING - FUNCTIONAL PRACTICE

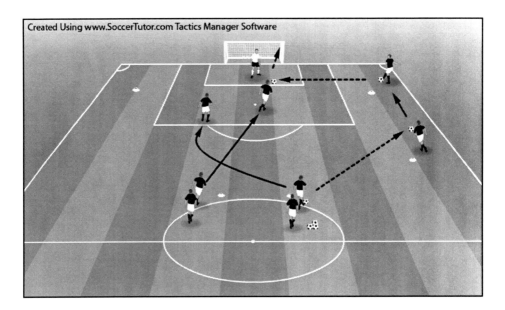

Created Using www.SoccerTutor.com Tactics Manager Software

In this simple functional practice we have pairs of strikers waiting in lines just outside the centre circle. There is a wide player positioned out toward one of the wings, in this case the right wing. The nearest striker to this winger passes the ball and they all begin to move forward.

As we have just discussed, we can use this functional practice to coach our strikers' movement as they attack the cross and try to score.

The strikers need to cross over as they move forward. The nearest striker should be dropping out towards the opposite wing and moving forward slowly while the furthest striker sprints to the near post.

Coaching this simple movement is great but why do our players cross over in front of each other?

This movement means the defenders have a decision to make and quickly. Do they mark the players and move with them or do they mark the positions and mark the player that moves into their space?

Just by making the movement we could be giving our strikers that split second advantage they need to convert a cross and score.

So now we understand the movement and the reason for it what might we say or coach?

What else might you add when you coach your players?

1. The furthest player needs to move late and fast toward the near post to meet any near post or driven cross ahead of the defender.

2. The nearest player should move away slowly towards the opposite wing but then back in again towards the back post. This should be done slowly to make sure they do not arrive in line, but slightly behind the other striker. For example, the striker attacking the near post should be in line with the six yard box and the second striker in line with the penalty spot.

3. Both strikers should hold their runs. Firstly, so they do not get ahead of the winger with the ball. Secondly, so they do not run too early getting ahead of the crossed ball.

4. The striker with the opportunity to score should attack the ball with only one thought in their mind. They need to want to score a goal more than anything else.

We are now getting into the realms of sport psychology which is something else you may want to learn more about.

How would you describe your striker?

Would you say they have a strong shot or that they are fast, or would you describe them as positive, aggressive, single-minded and fearless?

We need to look for certain traits in our strikers and not just technical ability.

The likelihood of getting hurt, the size of the defender and the speed of the ball when they go for a header should all be forgotten as they attack the ball to try and score.

Does this drill allow us to see these attributes in our strikers?

Not really. So how can we progress this functional practice to really test our strikers and see how much they want to score?

2 v 2 CROSSING - FUNCTIONAL PRACTICE

The first thing that we need to do is add defenders. Two of them can be positioned on the edge of the area waiting for the strikers to move.

With younger or less experienced players, we may want our defenders to be passive. However, with our older more experienced players we will need to add competition.

Can our strikers get ahead of the defenders and get to the ball first in order to get a shot away?

Have they the mental strength to get to the ball first and the will to score?

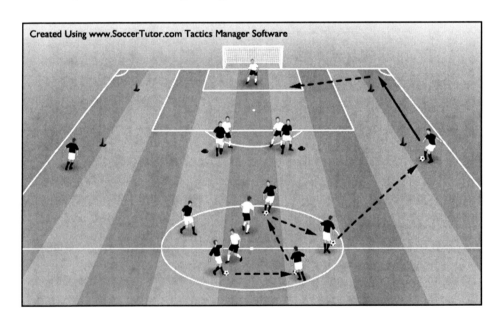

In this new functional practice we have again used the 5 attackers playing against 2 defenders within the centre circle. We can also use the same three passes rule as before; in this case they pass the ball to one of the wingers. The winger must then dribble or run with the ball beyond the end cone before crossing for the two central attackers to try and score.

The two central attackers start on the "D" of the penalty area as shown alongside the two defenders ready to attack the cross.

What is the advantage of using a functional practice in training?

We continually recreate the same scenario that we want to coach our players and try to improve. Here, we continually create crosses from both the right and left for our strikers to attack.

Let's have a quick think about our wingers in this drill and their tactical role within the game, receiving the ball and getting a cross played into the strikers.

What do you think we need to look for and therefore coach our wingers?

Firstly, the winger obviously needs to be ready for a pass from the central attackers in the centre circle. But how do we coach this?

Can they be on the half-turn, watching the players in the centre circle and anticipating any potential pass? Being in the "half-turned" position also means that they can see what's going on ahead of them.

Our wingers should always be in a clear position to receive a pass from the player with the ball.

The winger should keep moving as the ball is passed amongst the players in the centre circle to remain in an effective position. There should always be a clear route for the ball to be played to the winger, with no other players in the way.

What about speed?

Do they sprint down the wing to get to the byline quickly after they receive the ball?

Why?

This movement makes it difficult for any defenders to get back and help cut out the intended cross.

So now we have looked at our winger's position and our strikers runs to meet the cross but is there anything else we can coach?

Can you think of anything else we can coach?

What about the type of cross?

What types of crosses are there?

- The lofted cross.
- The cut-back.
- The driven cross.

How would you describe these three different crosses?

The lofted cross or high ball is intended for a striker to move onto and jump to head at goal. This is shown below as a cross to the far post.

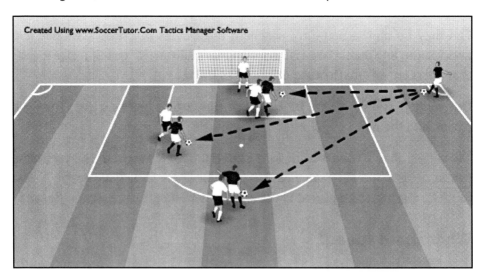

The cut-back is played behind the defenders who have run back, goal-side for an attacking midfielder or striker who has stood still or made a late run to create the space for a shot. This is shown above as a ball cut-back to the edge of the penalty area.

A driven cross is played in between the goalkeeper and the defenders at pace

for the attackers to sprint onto and deflect the ball into the goal. The driven cross is shown above as a ball played across the six yard box is met by the striker at the near post.

Can we use this functional practice to coach these crosses?

Yes of course, but let's think a bit more about what we want from our drill and the players.

The whole point of a functional practice is to practice the skill being coached within a game realistic scenario.

Let's think about our younger or developing players and their needs.

We really want lots of opportunities for our wingers to practice the crosses and our strikers shooting after reacting to them.

We don't really want the functional practice anymore; instead we only need to look at the cross and the striker's reaction.

To develop our players let's concentrate on the driven cross and think about how we can create a simple drill to coach our players.

Can you think of a simple drill which could be used to coach the driven cross?

What do we need to create our simple drill?

We simply need a goal, a player to cross the ball and a striker to run in and try and score.

SIMPLE DRIVEN CROSS SHOOTING - DRILL

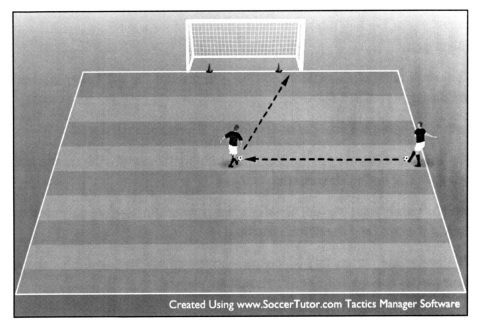

Created Using www.SoccerTutor.com Tactics Manager Software

So here we have a simple driven cross played across the front of the goal for the striker to run on to and shoot.

What are you going to coach?

Remember, we need to coach the two techniques and skills being developed.

Let's start with the driven cross, which means we need to coach the coaching points of the driven cross. These should be the same as a driven shot.

Can you remember the coaching points for a driven shot or cross?

1. *Approach* – The approach should be slightly from the side.

2. *Body Shape* – The standing foot is positioned next to the ball with the toes pointing across the goal, but with enough space to allow the kicking foot to swing through. The head should be steady, with the knee over the ball and

arms out for balance. With this driven cross our winger's body will need to twist round, thus enabling a low driven shot to be hit to the side instead of forwards.

3. *Contact* – The laces of the boot should make contact through the centre of the ball.

4. *Follow-through* – A swinging follow-through to the side but keeping low to keep the ball down. The follow-through also needs to be in the same direction as the cross to keep it accurate.

So, now we can coach our winger how to drive in a cross and have a drill that allows them to improve by repeating the process.

What about our striker? How and what might we coach them within this drill?

Shooting; more specifically the type of shot, as this will depend upon the position of the ball relative to them.

Was it the correct selection of shot or header and was it technically correct and on target?

Psychologically, did our striker want to score and put the maximum effort into scoring?

As the coach, we need to observe, evaluate and correct our players.

Can you think of any progressions for our simple drill?

- To try and promote shots into the corner of the goal we have added a couple of small traffic cones. Can the strikers score between the traffic cones and the goalposts.
- We could add a goalkeeper to make it more difficult to score.
- Adding a defender will challenge our striker's commitment and attitude. Making the defender passive to start with will help our younger or more inexperienced players.

Let's think about our attackers again; can we create a drill that allows them to try all these different types of shots? Can we also introduce more lofted crosses especially in a more competitive yet fun environment?

HEADERS AND VOLLEYS - FUN GAME

I propose an old favorite, headers and volleys.

Created Using www.SoccerTutor.com Tactics Manager Software

In our game we have a goalkeeper playing against our outfield attackers. The goalkeeper simply has to prevent goals being scored whilst the attackers can only score with a header or a volley.

Can we add competition?

We will challenge the outfield players to score five goals. To add competition we will give a goal to the goalkeeper for every ball they catch either from a cross or shot. Now we can play the game first to five goals.

Let's add to the challenge by giving goals to the goalkeeper for any shot that goes wide or over. This will increase the challenge for the outfield players as they shoot and hopefully improve their accuracy.

Can we motivate our players to try harder and create some fun?

We can increase the tension by swapping an outfield player with the goalkeeper each time the goalkeeper gains five goals first. The outfield player who gives away the fifth goal to the goalkeeper by shooting wide or allowing them to catch the ball from their shot or cross, then becomes the goalkeeper. If the outfield players get to five first the goalkeeper remains in goal for the next game.

Do we think that this game fits the challenge of creating a drill which allows more lofted crosses whilst adding a competitive element and making it fun. Can we however, use this simple children's game to increase the ability of our players and allow us to coach them.

Lets ask ourselves some questions.

Do our players get the opportunity to play lofted crosses, head at goal, shoot, try something new, little chip crosses, overhead kicks, swinging side on volleys and diving headers?

Yes. More importantly, all of it is based on what is going on around them. We have now added decision making. Can they get to the ball, adapt the shot and score.

Let's go back to our three crosses and what we have done so far. The driven cross drill can be used to coach the driven cross but also adapted to coach the lofted cross. We simply ask our winger to loft the cross rather than drive it.

By progressing onto our headers and volleys game we promote the lofted cross and chipped cross and our striker's reactions and ability to get to the ball, adapt to the position of the ball and shoot to score.

Let's move onto our third cross, the cut-back.

What do you think about this cross?

This cross is more game-related. The strikers need to run in on the goal taking the defenders with them. This is what creates the space behind them for the midfielders to run into and receive the cut-back cross.

So what drill can we use and how can we coach our cut back?

CROSSING - PHASE OF PLAY

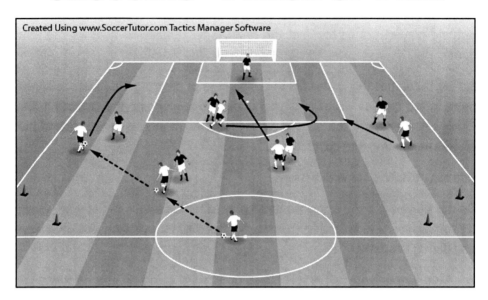

We need to use a phase of play. In this one, we have six attacking players and five defending players plus a goalkeeper. Our attacking team starts with the ball in the centre circle and play starts with a free pass to a team mate. The player with the ball can then join the attack, creating the 6 v 5 overload as they try to score in the full size goal.

In the diagram above, the defending team is given the chance to score by running the ball through either of the goals at each side of the half-way line. We can also see how the strikers have run in close to the goal. This is the movement that has created the space behind them which can be utilized by the winger and the midfielders.

We can now use this phase of play to coach our players to support the attack and look for this type of cross. The midfielders need to drive forward into this space, making sure the winger is aware of their movement. The midfielder needs to always be alert and ready to receive the ball as they will need to react quickly to the pass and get their shot away as soon as possible.

Should we just coach the one cross?

For younger players we might want to concentrate on the cross being coached, treating the phase of play a little more like a drill, preparing the movements. But as they get older and more comfortable we should use the phase of play as it should be, in a free flowing game.

This introduces game-speed and decision making, letting our players deliver whichever cross they feel will result in the best chance for a goal.

What can we coach?

- Decisions – Did they make the right choice of cross?
- Technique – Was the cross performed correctly and if not which coaching point caused the problem?
- Application – Did our strikers commit to the cross?
- Movement – Did our strikers and midfielders offer options?
- End product – Was our shot on target and if not why not? Which coaching point was wrong?

Let's think about our younger players who play mini-soccer, can we introduce a phase of play to them?

Of course, simply set your players out in the same team shape as they use in games.

7 v 7 MINI-SOCCER CROSSING - PHASE OF PLAY

Created Using www.SoccerTutor.com Tactics Manager Software

In this phase of play we are using three quarters of a full size mini-soccer pitch. We have a full-sized goal at one end and a target goal placed roughly on the edge of the penalty area at the opposite end. We also have two wide target goals in the form of cones, (shown bottom left and right). The pitch is split into thirds using marker cones; this is to make it easier for our younger players as they begin to learn more about positions and tactics.

Our attacking players line up with a deep midfielder or defender in the bottom third, three midfielders in the middle third and a striker in the final third. The defending team line up with a goalkeeper, a single defender in the final third marking the striker and two midfielders in the middle third.

The players should always start the drill in their designated third of the pitch as this will strengthen the player's perception of their positions on the pitch.

The phase of play begins with the deep midfielder, who first takes a touch out of their feet before playing the ball forward into a midfielder.

Due to the overload in favour of the attacking team they should always be in a position to play the ball forward. Remember, in this phase of play we only coach the attacking team.

So let's think about this phase of play and our players, what might your players do?

What do we want our players to do in this phase of play?

- Can they get the ball out to the wide midfielders?
- Can the wide player attack, dribbling forward into the final third before crossing?
- Can the wide player cross the ball?
- Can the attacking team get forward and attack the cross?
- Can they get back into positions after an attacking move breaks down and possession is lost?

With our younger player's we need to make sure we have the technical knowledge to be able to correct any mistakes.

Let's think again about our players crosses and the coaching points we need to understand and use as we coach.

Can you remember the coaching points for a driven cross?

1. *Approach* – The approach should be slightly from the side.
2. *Body Shape* – The standing foot is positioned next to the ball with the toes pointing across the goal, but with enough space to allow the kicking foot to swing through. The head should be steady with the knee over the ball and arms out for balance. With this driven cross, our winger's body will need to twist round enabling a low driven shot hit to the side instead of forwards.
3. *Contact* – The laces of the boot should make contact through the centre of the ball.
4. *Follow-through* – A swinging follow-through to the side but keeping low to keep the ball down. The follow-through also needs to be in the same direction as the cross to keep it accurate.

What about a lofted cross?

Can you think of the coaching points for a lofted cross?

1. *Approach* – The player should approach the ball slightly from the side.
2. *Body shape* – The player's standing foot should be slightly back and away from the ball. This should result in the player's kicking foot slightly reaching for the ball. The head should be steady and with the player's arms out to aid their balance.
3. *Contact* – The foot should make contact just under the centre of the ball. The contact on the foot should be at the top of the foot and at the base of the big toe.
4. *Follow through* – The player should have a big and high follow though to gain both height and power.

The cut back cross can be driven, in which case we can use the same coaching points as the driven cross. It could equally just be a simple side foot pass.

Can we remember the key points for a side foot pass?

1. *Approach* – Again, the player should approach slightly from the side giving them enough room to make a comfortable pass.
2. *Body shape* – The player's non-kicking foot should be placed next to the ball with the toe pointing in the direction of the intended pass. The head should be steady with arms out to balance the player.
3. *Contact* – The player's instep or inside of the foot should contact directly through the centre of the ball.
4. *Follow through* – The follow-through depends on the distance and helps both the guidance of the pass, its accuracy and the power.

Where do we go next?

Let's think about our better mini-soccer players or maybe our 11 a-side teams where they have a squad of 14 players turning up for training each week.

7 v 7 CROSSING - MINI-SOCCER GAME

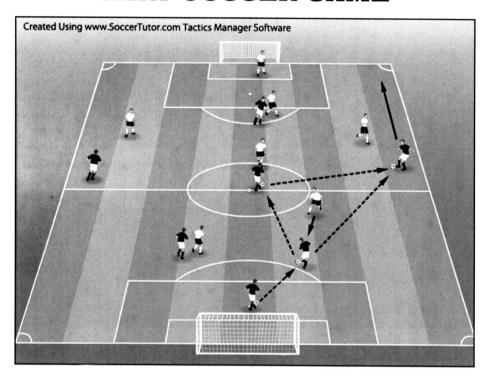

How can we use a free flowing 7 v 7 mini-soccer game as a tool for coaching crossing?

Simply add a rule.

Only a goal scored from a cross counts, anything else is not a goal and game restarts with a goal kick.

Our players are sure to utilise wide players and crosses at every opportunity if this is the only way they can score.

Whenever we use a mini-soccer game we need to make sure that our players get plenty of time to play. This will give them the chance to look for the opportunity to pass, shoot or move into a position to receive the ball.

Our players need to experience these different game situations so they can develop their creativity and decision making.

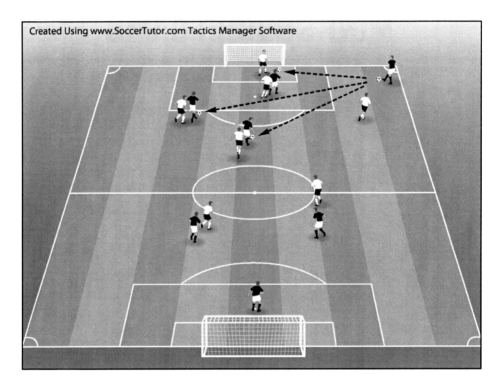

What else do our wide players need to practice?

We have looked at movement, the pass, the cross and the shot, coaching them all. However, it would be good to test our strikers a little more and challenge them to improve their finishing.

We have provided the free flowing headers and volleys game but we also need to force our players to provide all the different crosses for our strikers.

Let's think about our younger players again and a simple drill that provides all the crosses and the chance to react to them and shoot.

Let's start with the Simple Control Drill on page 78 and see if we can expand it into a drill for our strikers.

Remember, we simply need crossing opportunities and shooting.

CROSSING AND FINISHING - DRILL

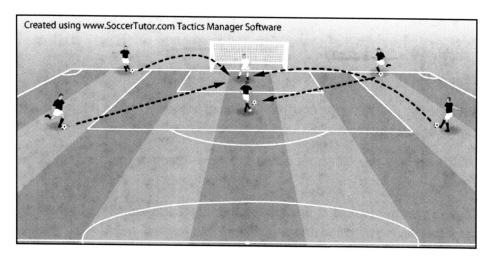

Let's expand the area and add a goal.

Our four players are pushed right out and are now positioned around the edge of the area with our striker around the penalty spot.

With our younger players we could simply allow our wide players to take turns crossing the ball, the first player crossing and then going one by one in a clockwise direction.

As an easy progression we can give them a number, 1 to 4, and the coach can shout the number for the corresponding wide player to cross the ball.

As the coach we need to make sure our crosses are varied; we need to see lofted, driven and cut-back crosses.

What other progressions could we use?

If we have two forwards in our team's formation let's use them both in the centre. Maybe we can challenge them both, who scores the most goals?

What are we looking for from our strikers?

- Mental Strength – Commitment and determination.
- Movement – Fast and direct.
- Shooting Technique – One touch finish – Accuracy and power.
- Control – If they need to control the ball, can they do it so they get a shot off with their second touch?

Is there anything else we should promote with our strikers?

How about agility and improvisation?

Let's use this drill to try the unusual. Overhead or bicycle kicks, back-heels, and diving headers just to name a few obvious ones.

Whichever way you can shoot is fine so long as it adheres to the rules of the game.

So now we have looked at the strikers and their finishing skills and the wide players receiving skills and crossing ability. What else is there?

We still need to look at our wide player and their dribbling skills.

Let's go right back to simplicity and think about a basic drill to get our younger players used to dribbling a ball with both feet.

We have all seen the simplest dribbling drill in the world. A line of players waiting for their turn to dribble a ball straight out round a number of cones and back again before passing the ball onto the next player who does the same.

Can you think of a few tweaks to improve it?

Can you arrange your drill so more players are active at any one time?

Can you manipulate the drill so your players are challenged to turn with the ball as well as dribbling?

Can you add fun and competition to the drill?

CHAPTER 5

Dribbling

SIMPLE SIDE ON DRIBBLING - DRILL

Created Using www.SoccerTutor.com Tactics Manager Software

Instead of lining three cones up in front of a line of players let's twist the line of cones through 90 degrees. We will also split the squad of players into four teams and set up each of them within four separate drills.

On the coach's command the first player in each team dribbles out and around the cones before passing to the next player in line to take their turn. The players always dribble around the cone furthest from the centre first, dribbling toward the centre.

Can you think of any advantages?

With the cones side on the players have to dribble out and then twist side on to dribble across and round the cones. Then they turn back again toward their team mates and pass the ball onto the next player in the line. This encourages our players to use the inside or outside of their feet to cut the ball around the first and last cones as they change direction.

Can you see any progressions?

SIDE ON MAYHEM DRIBBLING - DRILL

Created Using www.SoccerTutot.com Tactics Manager Software

This is the same drill set up as before, we have our four teams and four sets of side on cone drills. The difference is we will change the set of cones our teams dribble around.

Firstly, we have all our team's players dribble around the set of cones belonging to the team opposite, as you can see from the set of players on the bottom left of the diagram.

Can you see any problems?

Yes, as the players move to the opposite team's cones they have to dribble past the other teams player coming in the opposite direction.

As the coach we need to make sure our players concentrate on their own ball and dribbling and don't get drawn into kicking the other player's balls away.

Now we have our players focussed we can add competition and fun, but how?

Relay races. Our teams now compete against each other. Which teams players can dribble around their cones and back first?

Now we can challenge our players. Can they take small touches, keeping the ball under control enabling them to go faster?

Let's take another look at the diagram and the team top left. These players are shown dribbling around the full length of the two sets of cones opposite them and then back.

Please note, for this to work you need to have an odd number of cones so we have placed an extra cone in the centre of the two sets of three.

In this drill we now have two instances where our players not only have to dribble but also be watchful of players coming in another direction. These are at the start when they run out to the opposite line of cones, but also when they dribble across the cones as they meet another player dribbling in the opposite direction. We are now introducing 1 v 1 situations without the players actually realising.

Can you think of any other options?

Created Using www.SoccerTutor.com Tactics Manager Software

In the diagram above we can see players dribbling all the way along the two sets of cones nearest to them. Remember, again you will need to add a middle cone to make this work.

We also see the players dribbling around the cones of the team directly to the side of them. All of these different configurations of the drill can be alternated to keep the drill lively and interesting during the session whilst also introducing valuable 1 v 1 conflicts where players have to watch and avoid others.

So how many configurations can we think of?

- Each team dribbles round the three cones in front of them, their own cones. They can do this both ways.
- Each team dribbles round the cones of the team opposite.
- Each team dribbles round the cones of the team next to them.
- Each team dribbles round the cones of the team diagonally opposite them.
- Each team dribbles round all their cones and the team next to them.
- Each team dribbles round all the cones of the two teams opposite them.
- Each team dribbles round their own cones and then the cones of the team diagonally opposite. See diagram below left.
- Each team dribbles round all the cones starting with the cones directly opposite and finishing on their own cones. See diagram below right.

Let's look back at this chaotic dribbling drill and think about using it to actually coach and improve our players.

Can we use this drill to coach or will our players just learn through repetition?

Repetition will improve our players but if our players are not given advice or suggested options they will not improve. We need to offer our players the chance to learn through experience, but also through guided learning, question and answers, explanations and demonstrations. Our players learn in many ways and it is up to us as coaches to find the best way to individually coach our players.

When should we coach our players?

As this is an intense and competitive drill it would not be wise to stop halfway through a race. Let's use the natural break after each race to suggest improvements to our players which will allow them to go quicker.

So what can we coach?

1. *Positive attitude* – Our players need to be positive in their ability to dribble the ball.
2. *Technique* – Vision - Can the players get their heads up so they can see around them? If they look down at the ball they will not see the other players. Can we ask them to look ahead of the ball? This way they can see the ball out of the bottom of their eyes and the players around them out of the top of their eyes.
3. *Technique* – Footwork - Can your players use both feet as they dribble? They also need to make short sharp touches, they cannot let the ball get too far away from them otherwise they may lose control and time.

Let's get back to our current theme of dribbling. We have touched on 1 v 1 situations in this drill, but it is not really taking on and beating another player so let's think about introducing this challenge in another drill.

SIMPLE 1 v 1 CHALLENGE - DRILL

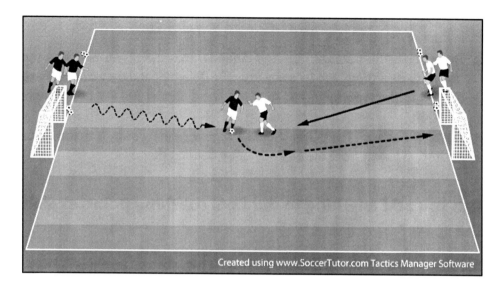

This is a very simple drill where we give our players the chance to take on an opponent, trying to beat them and get a shot in on goal.

Here we see two lines of players at each end of the playing area, which is approximately 20x20 but can be changed, dependent upon your player's ability. Each line of players takes turns as the attackers. On the coach's command to start we see the first black-shirted player in line dribble the ball into the area to take on the white-shirted player coming in from the right to defend their goal. The attacking player cannot shoot until they have got past the defender.

When all of the players in line have taken a turn attacking, the roles switch. The attacking players become defenders and the defenders now get their chance to attack.

This is obviously a great drill for our younger players and simple enough to logically go through the coaching points we need to explain, demonstrate and evaluate.

So can we think what the coaching points for dribbling

and taking on an opponent might be?

1. *Attitude* – Be positive, the player should take a positive first touch out of their feet and always believe they can beat the defender.
2. *Decision* – The player needs to decide on the "move" they will use to beat the defender before they get too near. This will avoid any dithering or confusion in front of the defender.
3. *Technique* – The distance from the defender that the player performs the "move" to beat them. Too far away from the defender and they will not have to react to the movement, too near and the defender has the opportunity to tackle.
4. *Exploit the space* – The player should always accelerate away into the space created and away from the defender after beating them.

Can you add anything to our final coaching point, exploit the space?

The attacker should also look at the path of his run when he accelerates away.

It is far better for the attacker to accelerate into the space behind the defender as this means the defender cannot get back to recover; this is because the attacker's body will be between the defender and the ball. If the defender does try and get back at the attacker there is always a possibility of the defender tripping them from behind as they both run in on goal.

This drill is obviously far too simple for our better players and we need to manipulate it to get more out of it.

Can we add competition?

Can we add pressure?

Can we add risk?

Can we add decision making?

Can we add fun?

How would you do it?

TEST YOUR DRIBBLING SKILLS
- SMALL SIDE GAME

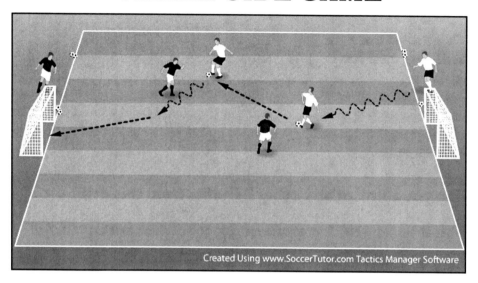

Created Using www.SoccerTutor.com Tactics Manager Software

This is more or less the same drill. The same area and the same lines of players at each end of the pitch are involved in this exercise.

We will add a challenge and competition by giving the first team five balls, in this case the white-shirted team to the right. They then challenge the opposition by dribbling the ball towards them and around them trying to score before the second of the two teams get their five chances to attack. However, this time the players have a decision, they have to choose the challenge or difficulty of the drill.

They can choose a 1 v 1 game, a 2 v 1 game or any of the various combinations listed below that they wish to choose.

How can we affect the choice, the pressure and the fun?

Let's give each scenario a different number of points. This means the more difficult the choice the better the reward.

Let's set out a sample set of rewards, you may want to alter these to best suit your players and their ability.

- 3 attackers vs 1 defender: 1 goal

- 2 attackers vs 1 defender: 2 goals
- 2 attackers vs 2 defenders: 3 goals
- 1 attacker vs 1 defender: 5 goals
- 1 attacker vs 2 defenders: 7 goals
- 1 attacker vs 3 defenders: 10 goals

Will this add fun?

The different rewards certainly add fun as the first team decides on the different options for each of their five attempts as they try to build a good score. The second team then has their turn trying to build a score higher than that posted by the first team.

Can you think of any other benefits from this drill?

What about team building, communication and decision making?

The pressure is on the players to perform but the team must take responsibility for their decisions.

How will you coach within this drill?

We need to point out the mistakes whilst explaining and demonstrating the correct technique but can we do it by stopping the drill?

No.

We need to continue rapidly through this fast-paced drill until all the teams' five balls and attempts are finished. Only after this can we step in and offer suggestions, coaching points and demonstrate improvements that might yield rewards for the players.

Let's use the natural breaks for players to recover and coaches to coach.

Thinking about what we have already read and learnt, let's take a look at our Striker's Movement Squad Drill on page 41.

Can we progress this drill to look at passing, receiving and dribbling?

MOVE, RECEIVE THEN 1 v 1 DRIBBLING - DRILL

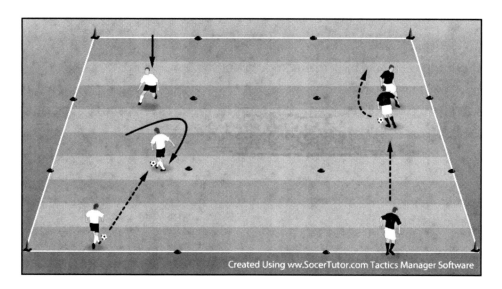

Created Using ww.SocerTutor.com Tactics Manager Software

As was the case before, we simply have our three players, one at each end and one working in the middle. The player at the bottom passes the ball into the middle player who moves to receive the ball.

Once they have the ball they can turn and run at the top player who moves toward them to defend the end zone and win the ball off them. The middle player's task is simply to take on the defender and dribble the ball around them and over the top line.

The players should all rotate positions after a number of attempts.

What would be good practice for our players prior to this drill?

Give all your players a ball each and let them practice their dribbling and more importantly their moves.

Can they drop their shoulders and fake a move, perform their scissors, step-overs, Mathews or 360 degree spins?

Can we think of a quick and easy environment for this practice?

Simply use a 20x20 area and throw down a few marker cones on the floor.

Ask the players to use the cones as defenders. Can they turn away with the ball, dribble around them or take them on whenever they dribble the ball up to one.

Quick and easy, now back to our "move, receive then 1 v 1 drill"

Can we use this drill to coach Passing, Receiving and Dribbling?

Of course.

Let's look specifically at the dribbling and the move or skill being used to take on the defender.

What are the coaching points that affect the success of the move?

1. *Attitude* – Be positive, the player should take a positive first touch out of their feet and always believe they can beat the defender.
2. *Decision* – The player needs to decide on the "move" they will use to beat the defender before they get too near. This will avoid any dithering or confusion in front of the defender.
3. *Technique* – The distance from the defender that the player performs the "move" to beat them. Too far away from the defender and they will not have to react to the movement, too near and the defender has the opportunity to tackle.
4. *Exploit the space* – The player should always accelerate away into the space created and away from the defender after beating them.

Let's progress the drill again, can we create a more game-realistic environment with a little more pressure on the receiving player.

4 v 4 HALF TURNED - SMALL SIDED GAME

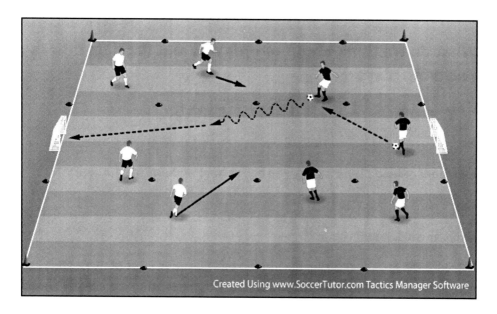

Created Using www.SoccerTutor.com Tactics Manager Software

Here we have a 4 v 4 small sided game set up in an area 40x30 with a few rules which promote dribbling and taking on an opponent. The pitch is split into four equal areas with the four players from each team split into pairs in each of their two end zones. These are the "starting positions" we will use to restart the drill. A target goal is placed at each end

At no point in the drill can the pairs of players in either end zone move from their zone.

To begin the drill, the ball starts with one of the two players in the very end zone. They take a touch out of their feet and look for a pass into one of their team mates in the adjacent zone. None of the players can leave their designated areas until the ball is received by this team mate.

The aim of the drill is for the player with the ball and their team mate to attack the opposite end zone and try and score in the target goal. The players are encouraged to take on the opposing team's players in the other middle zone.

Why do we make sure the players cannot leave their designated areas until after the pass is received?

This allows the time for our receiving players to get into space and be ready to receive the pass before being challenged by the defenders.

What do we think about our players and the pass into the receiving player?

Is the receiving player being challenged or marked by a defender?

No.

Can the receiving player receive the ball in front of them, half turned?

Yes.

Is this an advantage?

Yes, with the receiving player having the ball played in front of them, they can receive the ball facing forward, half turned. This means they are already turned to face the opposing players and can see everything ahead of them, they are also in a good position to move forward immediately.

In this way we promote the opportunity for our players to receive the ball and run or dribble forward very quickly.

How can we adjust the drill for our better or improving players?

We can always remove the central cones, making two ends zones and a larger central area, thus merging the pairs of players in the new central zone.

This change to the drill will add momentum and competition as the players are now allowed to compete in the central area.

What do we now think about our players and the pass into the receiving player?

It is now a lot more difficult for our players to receive the ball in front of them.

The receiving players will be marked more closely they therefore need to use a movement, a "show to go", to receive the ball ahead of them.

Otherwise they will need to use a "go to show" movement to receive a pass "safe side"

What is a "safe side" pass?

This is a pass that is played to the side of the player furthest from the nearest defender.

Let's think about a pass played "safe side", does it mean the winger cannot receive the ball facing forward, due to the ball being played behind them?

Can our player receive a "safe sided" pass half turned?

Yes.

If the ball is played safe side, the winger needs to sprint backwards and get to the ball with a good distance between them and the nearest defender.

If this gap is big enough the winger can get around the ball and receive it half turned facing the defender and in a good position to take them on.

Can we coach this movement in this drill?

Yes, but it will not be easy, especially when we consider our younger players.

So what do you propose for our younger players?

We will need to remove the defenders to start with. Then we need to create a passing sequence that forces our players into the movement and half turned position.

SIMPLE HALF TURN - DRILL

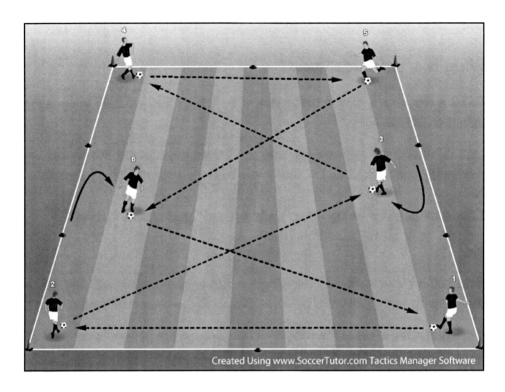

Created Using www.SoccerTutor.com Tactics Manager Software

Here, we have six players spread out around a rectangular playing area.

Make the area suitable in size for the players you are coaching.

What do we mean by this?

The distance between players needs to be a distance in which they can pass over easily, with an appropriate strength of pass and with accurately. The drill starts with a ball at the feet of the player bottom right who makes a first pass across the bottom of the area to the player bottom left. Importantly the receiving player should control the ball with the inside of their left foot.

Why?

Let's think about how they control the ball and their body shape. Controlling the ball with the inside of their left foot means they stop the ball directly in

front of their body and facing forward. This means they are looking forward and ready to make the next pass. If they control the ball with their right foot they will have to turn to face the passing player. This means they cannot see the whole playing area and therefore cannot see all the passing options there would be in a game.

The second pass in the drill gives our players the chance to practice receiving a "safe side" pass. The pass is played from the player bottom left to the player in the middle of the right hand side of the area.

What do you want to see from your receiving player?

Firstly, can they sprint back to the safe side pass, getting beyond the pass? This can allow the player to let the ball come across the front of their body, receiving the ball with the inside of their right foot, half turned and facing forward.

The third pass in the drill is up to the player (top left) who again needs to control the ball ahead of them.

For older or better players you may want to throw in a challenge. Remember to always think about your drill and different things to try.

Let's ask our better players if they can step into this third pass and chop it to their left with the outside of their left foot.

The fourth pass is from our player (top left) across the top of the rectangle to the adjacent player (top right).

What will we be coaching our player (top right) as they receive the ball?

It is the same as our player bottom left of the rectangle. They need to let the ball come across the front of their body and control it with the inside of their left foot, facing the playing area.

The fifth pass is played from the player top right into the player in the middle of the left hand side of the rectangle.

This is the second opportunity in the drill to practice and coach the movement and receiving skills needed to control a "safe side" pass.

What do you want to see from the receiving player?

Its the same movement and receiving skills as the player on the opposite side of the area. They should sprint back to the safe side pass getting beyond the pass, allowing the ball to come across the front of their body. This allows them to receive the ball with the inside of their right foot, half turned and facing forward.

The final pass is then played back to the player bottom right for the whole drill to start again.

What do we, as the coach, need to make sure happens in this drill?

1. We need to revolve our players around the positions to make sure they all get the chance to try the different receiving skills.
2. We need to change the direction of the drill, see below.

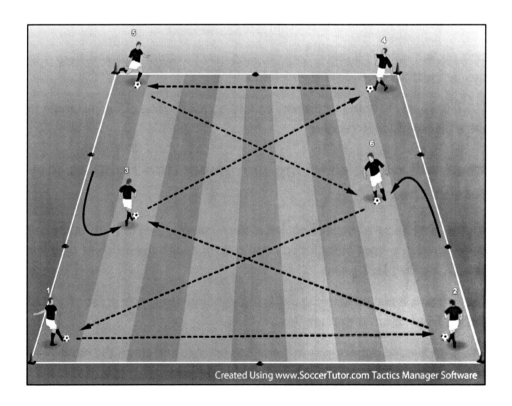

Why?

Our players need to be able to receive the ball with both feet. Going in the opposite direction will mean they need to let the ball come across their body in the opposite direction and receive the ball with the opposite foot.

The player bottom left now starts the drill by passing to the player bottom right who in turn passes into the player midway along the left hand side of the area.

So what about this new safe side pass into the player midway along the left hand side of the area.

What do we now want to see and coach?

Again, our players need to sprint back to the safe side pass, getting beyond the ball. However, this time the player needs to let the ball come across the front of their body and receive the ball with the inside of their left foot, half turned and facing forward. The next pass is into the player top right.

Now our players can receive the ball half turned and ready to dribble forward, let's have another look at our player's 1 v 1 dribbling skills.

Let's speed the drill up again and add some competition and fun.

Can we think of a way of adapting the "Two Goals Shooting Drill" on page 14 to incorporate a 1 v 1 challenge?

Have a look at the drill and see if you can adapt it before reading on.

TWO GOALS DRIBBLING - DRILL

Created Using www.SoccerTutor.com Tactics Manager Software

Here we see the same layout as before, with two neutral goalkeepers in two goals at the top of a 20x20 playing area. But this time the players are divided into two teams, black-shirted (bottom right line) and white-shirted (bottom left).

One of the players starts as a defender in the centre of the playing area, in this case a white-shirted player. The first player in the opponent's line, in this case the players bottom right, dribbles forward with the ball and attacks the defender and goal.

The drill is simply now a 1 v 1 challenge followed by a shot at goal.

But how can we add momentum?

How quickly can we get the next player dribbling and shooting whilst also adding a bit of fun and competition?

The fun and competition is easy, it's one team against the other. Which team scores the most goals?

What about momentum?

To continually rotate the players we simply ask the player shooting to become the defender after they shoot. The defender fetching the ball and rejoining his team's line of players is shown in the diagram below.

Created Using www.SoccerTutor.com Tactics Manager Software

The black-shirted player has turned after their shot to challenge the white shirted player now dribbling out toward the goal.

This drill can rotate very quickly so we need to keep an eye on when the next player begins to dribble out towards the new defender.

With the younger players the coach may need to call "go" or "start" to allow the next player to begin. With older or better players you may want to just keep an eye on the situation and actively promote speed.

Again, with this dribbling drill it is an environment for our players to practice

the challenge of beating an opponent and it is up to the coach to tweak this environment.

For younger players we can slow the drill down or ask the defenders to be a little more passive promoting success. Of course we do the opposite for our better player's speeding the drill up and increasing the competition.

When will we explain and demonstrate our coaching points in this drill?

Use the coaching points to stop the drill after a few minutes. This means the players can use the break as a short rest period, which also has the bonus of keeping our players fresher and prolonging the quality of the drill.

What were the dribbling 1 v 1 coaching points?

1. *Attitude* – Be positive, the player should take a positive first touch out of their feet and always believe they can beat the defender.
2. *Decision* – The player needs to decide on the "move" they will use to beat the defender before they get too near. This will avoid any dithering or confusion in front of the defender.
3. *Technique* – The distance from the defender that the player performs the "move" to beat them. Too far away from the defender and they will not have to react to the movement, too near and the defender has the opportunity to tackle.
4. *Exploit the space* – The player should always accelerate away into the space created and away from the defender after beating them.

Can we think of a fun environment for our players where they can practice close control, dribbling and shooting?

Does it always have to be a drill?

WEMBLEY - GAME

This is a simple game where every player is on their own, all trying to be the first to score. Any number of players can play this game; we just need a goal, goalkeeper and a ball. To keep everyone involved we will let all the players play until the first one scores five goals.

How is this going to challenge the players?

Ball control, shielding and dribbling skills will be challenged as every other player on the pitch tries to win the ball. Shooting skills will be improved as each player looks to shoot as soon as the opportunity arises.

As coaches, we need to let our players experience different situations allowing them to find their own solutions. We have to provide environments which allow our players to experiment and become creative. We need small sided games, phases of play, drills and games but we also need thinking coaches to provide these environments.

Let's get back to our more formal original shooting drill and progress it again, but this time for the one-two pass, dribbling and shooting.

THREE LINES DRIBBLING - DRILL

The players line up in three lines ahead of a goal and goalkeeper.

The drill starts with the first player in the line on the left side dribbling their ball through a number of cones and then firing off a shot at goal, shown above.

The player turns immediately after shooting to face the first player in the middle line. The first player in line then passes the ball into them and they provide the one-two pass back to them as they run forward to receive the ball and shoot at goal, shown in the next diagram.

The player from the first line (who had the first shot at goal) then joins the back of the middle line of players. The middle line player now turns immediately after shooting to face the first player in the third line. The first player in the third line then dribbles their ball forward and takes on the middle player in a 1 v 1 confrontation.

Can the player beat the defender and get a shot on target?

The player from the middle line then joins the end of the third line and the

player from the third line retrieves their ball before joining the back of the first line, shown below.

This is a nice drill that promotes all the attacking skills that we have seen so far, shooting, simple dribbling, a one-two and then the 1 v 1.

What else can we coach in this type of drill?

Our goalkeepers.

Remember to include them in your thoughts as a coach. Let's look at their movement as the drill moves from line to line and the positioning and stance of the goalkeeper as the shot is taken.

We are looking for short quick steps as they move, keeping their feet close to the floor at all times.

Why?

Their feet need to be close to the floor, with no jumping, so they are always able to dive up off the floor and out to make a save.

Can they move into line with the ball and down the line toward the ball to narrow the angle for the shot?

Coming back to our theme of dribbling, let's move on from the drills and into a free flowing small sided game.

What do we need to let our players practice within the game?

We need to let our players practice their receiving skills, half turned and facing the defender.

They need to be confident and explore options taking on the defender and dribbling around them.

Can we now think of a dedicated small sided game?

DRIBBLING END ZONES - SMALL SIDED GAME

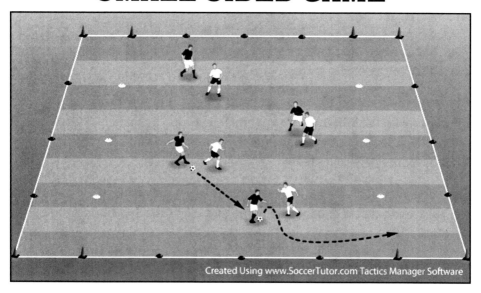

Created Using www.SoccerTutor.com Tactics Manager Software

Here we have a 4 v 4 small sided game set up in an area 40x30 with a 5 foot wide end zone at each end.

The players play 4 v 4 with the object of dribbling the ball into the end zone at the opposite end of the pitch.

Let's analyze this small sided game and think about our players and what they need to do to dribble the ball into the end zone.

Can we try and break down the skills and techniques required of our players into individual coaching points?

What is the first thing our players need to do and therefore what is the first coaching point?

Movement to Create Space

Can our attacking players use all of the area, expanding the play and opening up passing options for the player with the ball?

Can they use individual movements to create space for themselves to receive the ball?

What else might we say about creating space and player movement?

What about when our players are in a position to dribble at an opponent, what can we say to their team mates?

Our team mates need to keep wide and spread out. Any movement toward the player with the ball could prevent their intended movement. Even worse, it brings the defenders closer to the player with the ball and condenses the play, a bonus for the defending team.

Can our players look for 1 v 1 opportunities when they make their passes and can their team mates expand the game and allow the 1 v 1 opportunities to develop?

Now we should think about our dribbling player who has received the ball and sees the 1 v 1 opportunity.

What is our second coaching point?

Positive Attitude

Our players need to be positive and always believe they can beat the defender.

Now that our players have the right attitude what do they need to do to beat the defender in the 1 v 1 situation?

What is our third coaching point?

Decision making.

The player needs to decide on the "move" they will use to beat the defender before they get too near. This will avoid any dithering or confusion in front of the defender which will result in the defender being able to make a challenge.

Now our player is confident and knows what they will do to get round the defender we can look at our next coaching point, the technique of our player.

What would you list as key points of the player's technique?

Disguise

Can the player disguise the way they really want to go and fool the defender, unbalancing them as they trick their way past them? Can they drop their shoulder or use a "move" making a positive movement in one direction that will be followed by the defender? After the movement or disguise the player needs to move off in the opposite direction.

What about this change of direction, is there anything we would want to add as a further coaching point?

Exploit the space

Can our players show a change of pace, accelerating away into the space created and away from the defender after beating them? After beating the defender can they still be positive and speed away into the end zone?

Now we know the coaching points for our small sided game can we challenge ourselves to find another progression for coaching dribbling skills.

Can we think of a rule to promote dribbling in this SSG?

Let's steal a rule from Rugby Football, our players cannot pass the ball forward. This way, the only way to advance is to dribble or run with the ball.

Now let's take a look back through the book to see if there are any functional practices or phases of play we can adapt and utilise as a progression.

Whenever the functional practice or phase of play involves an attacking player and a defender it can be used with small tweaks or an instruction from the coach to improve dribbling whenever the chance arises.

Let's look at the crossing phase of play and see what we can do.

DRIBBLING OPPORTUNITIES - PHASE OF PLAY

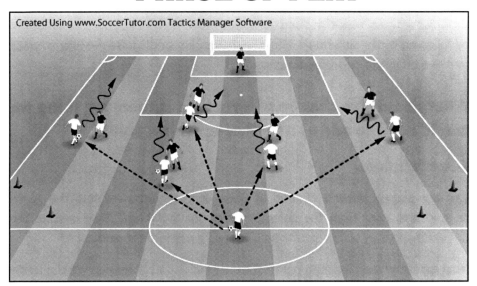

Created Using www.SoccerTutor.com Tactics Manager Software

Here we have the same crossing phase of play with the players in the same positions and the same passing options.

As the coach we need to promote a positive attitude within our players and ask them to take on an opponent when the opportunity arises. We do not want them to pass or cross first time, we want them to take on a player and go towards goal or down the line.

Let's look a little closer at the phase of play and our players. We want to consider the creating space coaching point.

Would we say that all our players have created space?

I think from the diagram we can say yes, but I will now ask a slightly different question.

Would we say our players have created space to receive the ball?

What do we think about our wide left sided player?

They are in space and a "go to show" move would certainly move the defender away before they sprint back to receive the ball half turned; but have they run back into a position where the player with the ball can actually pass to them?

The player with the ball will find it difficult to pass the ball as the more central left sided player is actually in the way of the pass.

Remember to watch and comment or question your player's movement to create space.

Stop the game quickly and ask your player, have you actually created space to receive the ball or just created space?

Let's pick on another coaching point, this time the decision.

We have always referred to the decision as the type of move the player will make to take on the defender. We need to make our players aware in a phase of play or small sided game that there is more to this decision.

What else should we consider?

We need our players to think about the players' game-environment. Are they actually in a good position to dribble at and take on a defender?

Is it a 1 v 1 situation that could lead to a goal scoring opportunity or chance to cross?

Our players need to be confident and attempt to beat players but let's make sure they are aware of the game environment and therefore the best options.

Let's take a look at the next diagram, which shows the play unfolding in our dribbling opportunities phase of play. The ball has been played out wide to the left sided player.

The player has attempted to come short for the ball but the defender has come with them and is close enough to tackle.

As the defender applies tight pressure to the player with the ball; both the supporting and balancing defenders close in.

The receiving player now has a problem.

Let's have a look at the situation below, what do we think?

Who can offer support and passing options for the player with the ball?

Where is the space on the pitch?

Where does the attacking team need to move the ball?

If the defenders move toward the ball to add pressure and confine the play then the attacking team has to move the ball out and spread the game again quickly.

Can they switch the ball to the right?

The nearest player needs to drop off deep and offer as support to the player with the ball. They should receive the ball on the right foot, back foot and switch it across to the right hand side of the pitch.

Can we replicate this in a drill?

CHAPTER 6

Switching Play

DROP OFF AND SWITCH PLAY - DRILL

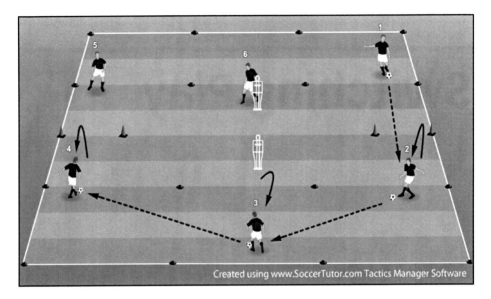

Created using www.SoccerTutor.com Tactics Manager Software

In this drill we can see our six players spread around the playing area, make the area suitable to the strength and quality of your players.

There are a couple of mannequins for the two central players to play off and a couple of coned gates for the two sets of end players.

The ball starts with the player at the top right of the playing area. The player passes the ball straight down to the player opposite. The receiving player should move toward the coned gate and then drop off to receive the ball on the back foot. This allows them to pass the ball across to the central player.

The central player should start against the mannequin and then drop off to receive the ball facing forward.

The ball can then be passed over to the player bottom left; they then move forward through the gate before dropping back off to receive the ball.

The ball can then be played directly opposite and across the three players at the top of the drill. These players duplicate the same movements and receiving skills as the players below, see the diagram below.

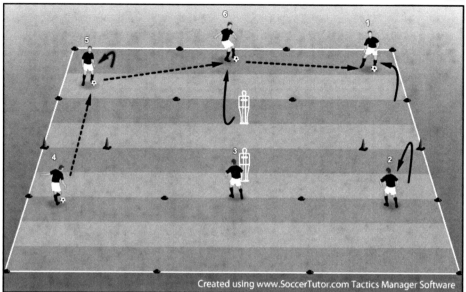

Created using www.SoccerTutor.com Tactics Manager Software

What are we looking for in this drill?

If we remember the phase of play, there were a number of questions. We asked about the support, passing options and switching the ball from one side of the pitch to the other.

This drill allows our players to practice moving off the defender to provide a passing option. It also allows the players to switch the ball quickly across the pitch.

What progression might we add?

Do our players always pass the same way across the pitch?

No

As the coach, let's introduce the command: switch. When the coach shouts the command the direction of passing should change; in this case from clockwise to anti-clockwise.

What about our younger players? Can we simplify the drill to just concentrate on the passing and receiving skills of switching the ball.

SWITCHING PLAY - CIRCLE DRILL

Created Using www.SoccerTutor.com Tcatics Manager Software

Here we have our players positioned in a circle and a ball being passed around in an anti-clockwise direction.

The players should let the ball come across their body, trapping the ball with the inside of their furthest foot from the passing player, in this case the right foot.

Can we think of a progression?

Again, we can use the "switch" command to keep the players on their toes and swap the direction the ball is passed, but is there anything else we could do?

We could start the drill with two balls. Start with them at the feet of two players opposite each other.

What about adding some fun?

Can the players keep both balls moving?

Can they get the second ball to catch the first?

Who is in possession of the first ball when the second one gets to them as well?

Let's take another look at switching play and try to give our players the chance to repeat the tactic, but in a more game-related environment.

Can we think about a functional drill but for our younger players?

What do we need from our functional drill?

We want to get the ball from one side of the pitch to the other to capitalise on the free space that opens up when a defence shifts across.

We need our players to practice the movement coming off a defender and dropping off to receive the ball facing forward.

We need the drill to be game-realistic so let's use the attacking third of the pitch.

We need players across the whole width of the pitch, so let's have two central players and two wide players, one wide left and one wide right.

We need to allow our players to repeat switching the play but without any pressure, no defenders.

We need to give an end product to reward the play, so we will add a goal and goalkeeper.

To finish the drill we will try and add crossing and shooting.

SWITCHING PLAY TO CROSS - FUNCTIONAL DRILL

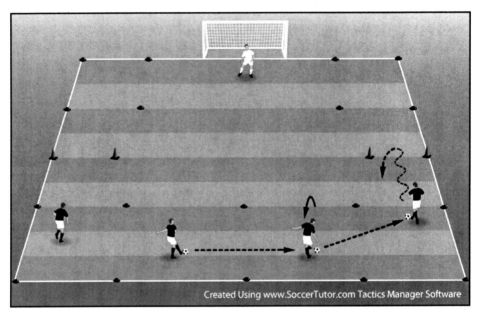

Created Using www.SoccerTutor.com Tactics Manager Software

Here we have four players spread across the pitch, the ball starts with one of the central players, in this case the centre-left player.

The player passes the ball across to the right wing via the other central player. The central players should start on the more advanced cones and check back to receive the ball, which is passed safe side, facing forward and on the back foot.

The ball is then passed out wide to the right winger who dribbles towards the gate positioned 5 or 10 yards ahead of them. All the players should move forward at this point. The winger, pretending the gates are defenders, should turn and lay the ball back across the pitch to the player inside right who has checked back to receive the ball.

The ball is then passed back across the pitch to the left winger who can then dribble forward with the ball beyond the final cones before crossing.

The two central players can then make crossing runs forward, just as we coached earlier, and the right winger can make a supporting run to the edge of the box as they try to score.

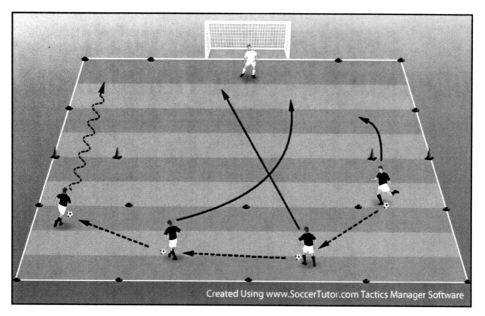

The diagram above shows the ball being played to the left and the runs from our strikers.

Can we remember the speed and type of runs needed?

The furthest striker should sprint toward the near post as soon as the crossing players head comes up.

The nearest player moves across and then forward in a slower more semi circular type movement aiming to arrive around the far post. The player should also arrive a good few paces further back and not in line with the other striker.

The last player should aim to support diagonally back from the back post and further back again.

What else might we say about the drill?

Don't forget to practice switching the ball in both directions. This means we need both central players taking turns to start the drill, sending the first pass in different directions.

Can we now progress our functional practice?

SWITCHING PLAY WITH DEFENDERS - FUNCTIONAL DRILL

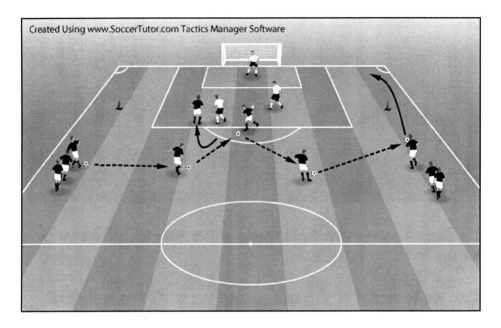

Created Using www.SoccerTutor.com Tactics Manager Software

Here we see our progression; two defenders have been added and we see a bit more structure to our team formation: two strikers and a midfield four. You could change this formation to match your own team structure.

The ball starts with the first player in the line on the left. The ball gets played across the midfield and then into the striker, before being bounced to the second midfielder and across to the opposite winger.

What can we coach in this drill?

Passing, creating space, striker movement, crossing, shooting and the goalkeeper can all be coached.

Remember to always think about your players and their skill levels. How many different skills can they cope with and therefore how much can you coach?

Let's think about the strikers movement.

What can we say about the movement of the two strikers in the diagram?

The nearest striker has moved toward the ball and then peeled away leaving the second striker to run forward, receive the ball and pass it back to the second midfielder.

You can now use this drill to introduce the dummy to your players.

What do we need to say about the dummy?

For younger players the dummy needs to be called by the second player as they can see the dummy is on, or able to be performed. They need to take the initiative and make the decision, otherwise the first player will bounce the ball back to the midfielder.

Is this a good drill to coach the new dummy movement to our players?

What about are less experienced players?

Can we think of an easier environment to coach the dummy?

Let's try and use a simple drill rather than a functional drill or phase of play. We also need to reduce the number of players involved in the play to focus them on the particular skill being coached.

How many players do we need to perform the dummy?

We only need three players. One to pass the ball and one to dummy the ball with a further receiving player behind them.

In theory we could go back to our simple three players in line drill from page, but lets try and introduce a bit of movement and flow to our drill.

Can we progress the switching play - circle drill we used at the start of this chapter.

DUMMY THE BALL - CIRCLE DRILL

Created Using www.SoccerTutor.com Tactics Manager Software

Once again we have our players positioned in a circle, but this time we start with two players in the centre of the circle and the ball at the feet of a player on the outside circle.

The drill starts with the designated player in the centre who is going to perform the dummy. This player should make a movement toward the player with the ball showing for the pass. The second player in the middle should make a movement to position themselves behind the first player, creating the opportunity for the dummy.

The starting player on the circle can then play the ball through the legs or past the "dummying" first player in to the second player who receives and controls the ball.

The "dummying" player then turns to show for a return pass, before playing it out to another player on the outside circle. They then follow their pass out of the circle and they join the players in the outside circle, shown in the diagram below.

Created using www.SoccerTutor.com Tactics Manager Software

The second player who remains in the centre is joined by the starting player as they should have followed their first pass. This now makes two players in the middle again and the ball at the feet of another player on the outside circle. The drill can now begin again with the receiving player becoming the "dummying" player and the starting player becoming the receiving player. See diagram above.

This drill can now revolve through all the players. Each time a passing player follows their pass into the middle they become the receiving player for the next drill. They then change to the "dummying" player in the second and then follow their pass back out to join the players on the circle again.

How can you make sure your players understand the movements?

Lets walk our players through the drill moving the ball and players as we go. Do this for a couple of phases and gradually speed it up until they all understand.

Lets now take this back into a more game related drill whilst also trying to progress our last functional drill.

6 v 5 SWITCHING PLAY
- PHASE OF PLAY

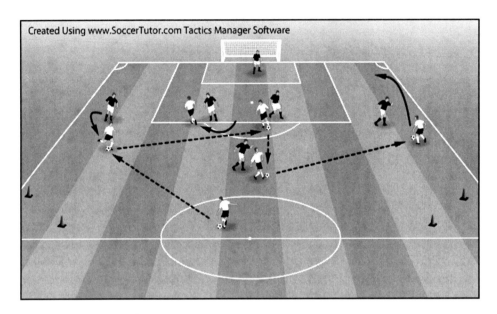

Created Using www.SoccerTutor.com Tactics Manager Software

Here we have the same 11-a-side phase of play layout that we have used before. Half a pitch is used with a full-sized goal at one end and two target goals placed by the half-way line, one in each corner. We then set our teams up with two strikers and four midfielders: three across the pitch and a defensive midfielder who starts the drill. These players attack the full-sized goal defended by a goalkeeper, four defenders and a midfielder. The wide midfielders are told to push wide and forward to engage the full backs.

As the coach, what are we looking to spot in this free flowing phase of play?

The trigger point in this drill which allows us to coach switching the play comes when the attack breaks down as a wide midfielder comes up against a full back.

As the coach, what are we looking to see from our team when this occurs?

Do they turn and play the ball out across the pitch, switching the angle of attack to the opposite side of the pitch?

Do the attacking players make the most of switching the play and attack down the opposite wing to cross?

Did they switch the play quick enough, catching the defensive team pushed across to the opposite side?

Created Using ww.SoccerTutor.com Tactics Manager Software

As the coach, what are we looking to see from our players?

Does the holding midfielder push forward to support the attack and do the strikers move to create passing opportunities?

Do the players receive the ball with an open body, facing forward so they can see the game environment ahead of them and maintain the momentum of the attack?

Do our players make the correct decisions to pass, dribble or shoot and just as importantly do they do it quickly?

Do our players take responsibility do they feel they can be creative and try something different?

Do they communicate to each other?

Obviously with our younger players we would concentrate on just one of these points, but how?

Let's take a closer look at some of these questions and what we can do as a coach to help our players understand them and therefore improve.

To help our younger or less experienced players and keep them focussed on the receiving skills theme of the session we could precede this game with one of our half turn drills. For these players it is important we plan out our session with a single theme. Looking just at this skill during the session and initial drill, we can then progress and stop the game when we see an opportunity to go over and demonstrate it again to our players.

What about our players decision making?

For our players to make the right decisions they need to be able to make mistakes, as long as they learn from them. They also need to make that perfect pass or run and learn from them. Basically we need to let our players play the game and learn from the games they play. We can then compliment their game with questions and comments.

How do you feel about that pass or run?

Was there something else you could have done?

Then we keep our players thinking about what they did in the game and hopefully they can learn from it.

What about our players taking responsibility and being creative?

This is down to you as the coach. Can you create a positive environment in which your players our happy to try new things and experiment. Be positive and encourage your players.

As we talk about taking responsibility and being creative would it be an issue if one of our midfielders took the opportunity to shoot as the ball is switched?

No, these are long range shots and something we have not discussed or developed as a drill so far, so let's take the opportunity to take a look.

LONG RANGE SHOOTING
- SMALL SIDED GAME

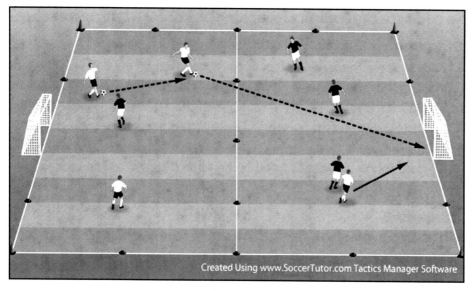

Created Using www.SoccerTutor.com Tactics Manager Software

Here we have another 4 v 4 small sided game, this time with a single full size goal at each end of the 40x30 playing area. We also have a half-way line which helps split the teams, both with three players in the defensive half and one striker in the attacking half.

How does this promote long range shooting?

We have a 3 v 1 overload in each defensive half. This allows these players the chance to work a shooting opportunity whilst the striker has to work very hard to create space against the three defenders.

With this simple small sided game our players should easily work long range shooting opportunities so what are we going to coach?

Do we need to coach creating a shooting opportunity?

With our younger players, we may want to simply reiterate that they should shoot whenever they have the opportunity. But we do not need to coach a move or pass to robotically create a shooting opportunity.

Remember the purpose of a small sided game is to promote creative and experienced players who learn through play. So let's leave our players to work the chance to shoot and then stick to coaching the actual technique of the skill as and when required.

So what are the technical coaching points for a long range shot?

1. *Approach* – The approach should be slightly from the side.
2. *Body Shape* – The standing foot is positioned next to the ball with the toes pointing towards goal, but with enough space to allow the kicking foot to swing through. The head should be steady, knee over the ball and arms out for balance.
3. *Contact* – The laces of the boot should make contact through the centre of the ball.
4. *Follow through* – A low strong follow-through to keep the ball down. The follow-through also needs to be in the same direction as the shot to keep the shot accurate.

What type of shot is it that we are coaching? A chip, a driven shot or a simple side foot passing shot?

These points listed should result in a technically good driven shot. If we want to coach a chipped shot we can look at the long range, lofted passing drills for the coaching points and differences.

We have now taken a look at long range shooting. This is an integral part of switching play and looking to create a shooting opportunity. But what else do our players need to do as they look to switch the point of attack.

Can we just pass the ball to a teammate?

How do we know they are ready to receive the ball?

Let's think about our players communication, how can we coach or promote communication?

It would be easy to say in any drill that you cannot pass unless the player you pass to has called for the ball but that is still a forced rule.

Is there a drill you can think of that really needs communication?

COMMUNICATION - SMALL SIDED GAME

Let's use a simple 5 v 5 small sided game with goalkeepers but with a twist, every player is wearing the same coloured bib.

The players are split into two teams of five and told to get together and sort out their positions and tactics. This time should also be used by the players to make sure they are aware of their team mates.

The two teams are shown in the diagram above as A1 to A5 playing B1 to B5 in a normal 5 a-side game

This drill promotes communication as the team mates of the player with the ball have to move into position and call for a pass.

Can we think of any other advantages of using this drill?

What about the player with the ball?

They need to play with their head up, checking the playing area to see which team mate calls for the ball and who is in the best position for a pass.

Why else would they need to keep their heads up?

They also need to check that its one of their team mates calling for the pass.

What would you do if you had eleven players at training instead of the ten needed for this small sided game?

We could add him as a floating neutral player but what about simply playing 6 v 5?

Are teams always equal?

No, a player could get sent off. It is always a good idea to make sure your players are prepared for every eventuality and this means playing an uneven game.

Let's continue with the small sided games and think of how we can promote switching play within this type of game.

We need to promote width and the idea of attacking down one side before switching across to the opposite side to attack again.

To make it easier for the attacking team we will add a floating player who makes a 5 v 4 overload in favour of them.

But how will we promote switching the play?

SWITCHING PLAY - SMALL SIDED GAME

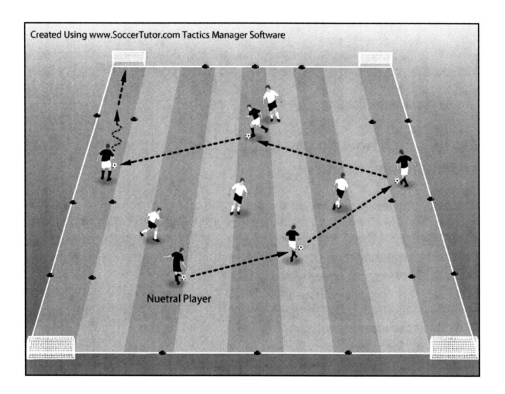

Created Using www.SoccerTutor.com Tactics Manager Software

Nuetral Player

Let's base our small sided game on a simple 4 v 4 without goalkeepers, adding two wide channels with target goals at each end of the pitch. The teams line up 4 v 4 but with the extra neutral or floating player to give a 5 v 4 overload to the attacking team.

Let's think about how we have the game set out and how we can use it to promote switching play.

How can we force our players to switch the point of attack?

We will add a simple rule. The attacking team need to pass the ball into a player positioned in one of the wide channels, or dribble it into the channel, to allow them to score in the opposite channel goal.

So in the diagram above we see the black shirted players attacking the two top goals. They play the ball out wide, passing to a player in the right channel. This opens the goal top left allowing them to switch play back across left for a shot.

As they have also passed across into the left channel they have now opened the right hand goal, so should the opportunity to shoot be blocked they can always switch back right.

How can we progress the drill, adding to the difficulty?

Simply remove the floating player to play 4 v 4.

As the coach how do you think this will impact the players and challenge them?

Obviously one less player means the defending team can go man to man.

The attacking team and specifically the player with the ball now needs to open their body, keep their head up and look for options. Maybe they need to dribble at another defender to create space or take them on.

The attacking team and more specifically the players without the ball need to work on their movement, can they "go to show" or "show to go" in order to create space for a pass.

We as the coach, need to look for all these technicalities as we observe our players during the game. If we see a problem with the movement of the players or we notice them with their head down for example, we need to step in and explain, coaching our players.

Can we also think about their movement not just to create space to receive a pass but also to create width.

What advantage does creating width add to an attacking team?

It is always easier to defend a compact team. A team that uses width spreads the defenders and therefore the spaces between them which can be used for a pass.

Can we show this to our younger players in a game related environment?

7 A-SIDE SWITCHING PLAY - PHASE OF PLAY

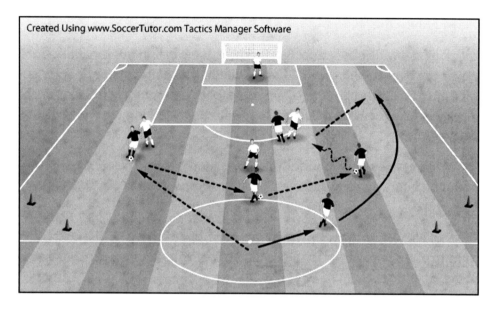

We can use half of our mini-soccer pitch and again set up two wide goals on the halfway line for the defending team to attack, should they gain possession of the ball.

The attacking team start with a standard 7 a-side formation with one striker, three advanced midfielders spread across the pitch and a holding midfielder or centre back who starts the phase of play.

Our defending team starts with a goalkeeper, one deep defender and two midfielders.

Why have we created such a big overload in midfield 3 v 2 and then 4 v 2? Should the holding midfielder move forward?

With our younger players we want to promote success. We want them to see the advantages of spreading the play.

How and what can we coach using this phase of play?

Let's start by keeping our holding player back. If we need to, we can put a line across the pitch as a visual aid to prevent the player advancing.

Now we can promote attacking interplay going forward and across the pitch with our three midfielders.

Let's look at a wide player dribbling inside with the ball. In this case our central player can overlap and provide further width. If a central player dribbles out wide, then that wide player can drive inside to support centrally, this movement may even take the wide defender away with them, leaving the wide channel free to exploit.

The holding player can support all this movement by always being in a defensive position, communicating and showing as an escape route to play the ball back and central.

This will also allow them to switch the point of attack easily. The midfielder turns to play the ball back to the holding player who can then pass out across to the other side.

Do you think we can progress this drill?

We can allow our holding midfielder to move forward and join the phase of play in a more attacking position.

What does this mean for our attacking team?

It obviously makes it easier for them with the overload increasing to 4 v 2.

But can you think of any problems or possible coaching points?

How do we think this overload will affect the way our attacking team plays?

We can assume they become more confident and attack minded which could result in other issues.

The team is now less likely to think about defensive duties and more likely to all

go forward leaving space behind them.

A single interception, tackle, lucky bounce or deflection could now result in a goal as the defending team now suddenly has the opportunity to get the ball in behind the attacking team with no cover to stop them.

We do not want to restrict our players interplay and movement so what do we need to do?

We need to introduce tactics and responsibility to our players.

The four midfielders need to take responsibility individually and collectively to keep one player in the central holding / defensive role. This will maintain defensive cover whilst allowing the point of attack to be switched through them.

Let's look at the diagram again.

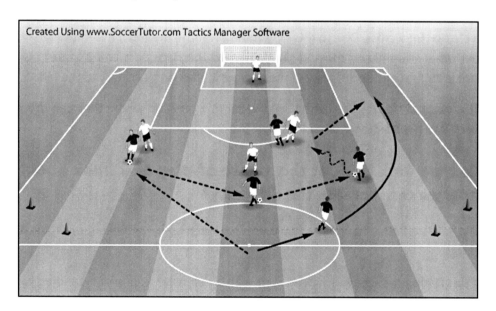

Created Using www.SoccerTutor.com Tactics Manager Software

What will we say if the holding player pushes on, as in the diagram, overlapping on the right hand side as the right sided player dribbles in towards the opponent's goal.

What will we say about our players' movements?

We need to allow our players to make their own decisions as the play unfolds, only afterwards can we suggest movements and promote ideas or tactics.

Why?

Our players may actually understand and be competent and so we need to know our players and only coach what is actually needed. We need to coach smartly and not in a repetitive fashion from a list of coaching points.

Going back to our younger or more inexperienced players what might we suggest as movement for our players?

If our wide midfielder drives in towards the goal, then the forward should move aside for two reasons. Firstly, they need to move out of the way of the attacking winger and secondly, as discussed before, they may even take the defender with them.

The overlapping holding player has obviously moved forward so there is now a chance for a cross. Due to this we should promote the movement forward of our other wide player moving slowly toward the back post and possibly our striker to turn and sprint toward the near post after drifting away to the left.

This naturally leaves the central midfielder in a position where they can drop back into the holding role and support the attack.

Can we look back at this phase of play and think about how we can increase the difficulty?

The easy way is to change the two teams to match up in midfield, three against three.

If this is too much maybe we can start with a defensive midfielder standing by the attacking teams holding player. They are then allowed to join the phase of play as soon as the holding player plays the first pass. This will at least mean there is a simple first pass to start the phase of play.

Let's move on again and change this 7 a-side phase of play into a more complicated 11 a-side phase of play to progress coaching switching play.

8 v 8 SWITCHING PLAY
- PHASE OF PLAY

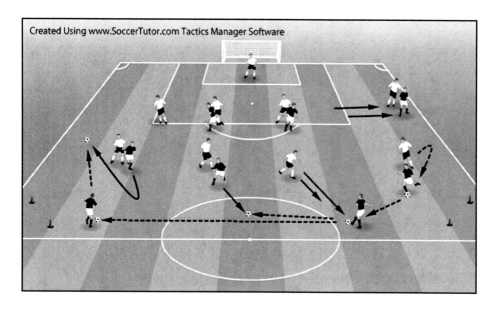

Created Using www.SoccerTutor.com Tactics Manager Software

Again, we use half a full size pitch and add a couple of wide target goals on the half way line.

In this phase of play we have three attacking strikers, three midfielders and two attacking full backs attacking the full-sized goal. The defending team lines up with a goalkeeper, four defenders and four midfielders.

The three strikers need to try and keep all four of the defenders occupied through their movement, allowing the three attacking midfielders and two full backs to push on against the four defending midfielders.

For our younger or more inexperienced players we need to force the opportunity to switch the ball so that we can, in turn, assess and coach what we see from the results.

The ball first needs to be played to an attacking full back. In this case the right back, who then tries to go forward. The defensive midfielder blocks the way and any pass forward which forces the right back to turn back and infield. This creates the opportunity to switch the play, switching the point of attack.

Have we seen our players switching the ball like this before?

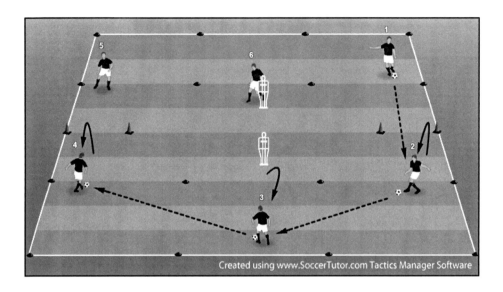

Created using www.SoccerTutor.com Tactics Manager Software

Drop off and Switch Play is the very first drill in the chapter and exactly mirrors what are players should be doing.

What did we coach in the drill?

Support for other players, passing options and the switching of the ball from one side of the pitch to the other.

Can we expand on this to give us some coaching points for this part of the phase of play?

- The players need to move off the defender quickly to provide a passing option.
- They also need to look at receiving the ball facing forward allowing them to switch the ball quickly across the pitch.
- We also need to look at the pass: are they played to the safe side?
- What about our players technique, can they receive and pass in two touches or even turn their body as the ball comes across them to pass across with one touch?

Remember, whenever we are coaching a phase of play, break down the things we want to look for and coach. We should let the play unfold, waiting for the chance to highlight and coach the theme of the session, in this case switching the play.

Please use these phases of play simply at first as you build up your experience and confidence.

Let's think about the phase of play again and what we are coaching. Can we challenge ourselves as coaches to ride with the game as it unfolds and keep on top of it.

Does switching the play mean that the ball has to go all the way from one wing to the other?

No, it is simply switching the point of attack to find a way forward.

Does the switch always have to start from a winger or wide player?

No, the important thing is that a player should not blindly push on in one direction until they lose the ball. They need to turn away from the problem and look to rework the ball in another attacking direction.

The phase of play adds this new dimension to our coaching. Our players can use the game to discover the options, learning when to turn away from an attacking move before it breaks down. Can they make the correct decision of when to recycle the ball, passing back and across the pitch? More importantly can a player take the initiative and be creative, finding the right time and pass to create a goalscoring opportunity?

Now that we have seen how using a phase of play develops our players let's take a few pages to see how we can use it to develop us as the coach.

Remember, with younger players we need to stick with one theme, for example here we concentrate just on the technique of switching the play. However with older or better players we need to be better coaches who understand the bigger picture. This means everything involved with the phase of play and the wider topic, which in this case is attacking and recycling the ball to attack again.

Let's take another look at this phase of play and see if we can work out a few scenarios that will give us more confidence to tackle coaching this and other phases of play.

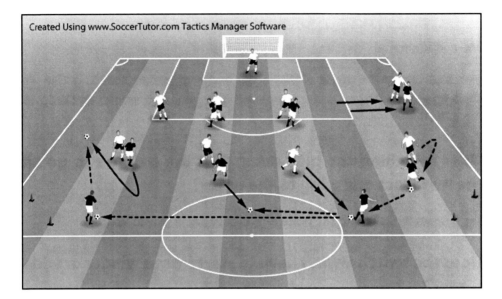

First of all we should look at the switched ball we see in the diagram, this is where the ball has been turned out and played all the way across to the left hand side of the pitch.

We will start by looking for a drill earlier in the book that simulates the situation and of course gives us the bite-size view of what we want to see next and the coaching points. This will again help us as coaches to develop our understanding of the connections between drills and games and more importantly the points that affect the success.

What drill can we use?

With the ball now out wide on the left we are actually in a progression of the Crossing – Phase of Play on page 117 which was a 6 v 5 phase. But to really break it down and find the coaching points we need a functional drill to helps us.

We now have a choice of drills that we can read up on, or better still we have coached before, that provide knowledge and experience to tackle this phase of play.

The team tactic of recycling and switching the play means we now want to exploit the space on the opposite wing. We can attack down this wing and look for a cross into the forwards. Drills which can help now include.

These are just a few of the many drills that could help, but lets think about it. Let's not get worried, many of the coaching points are similar and just need tweaking to the skill being coached.

Also, if we look at all the drills and all of the relevant options it naturally follows that this is simply a standard phase of attacking play. This means that the same layout can be used simply to coach many different skills and techniques to our younger players. We simply set a starting position and a pass that forces the ball where we want it to go. This targets the opportunity to attempt the skill during open play, watch it, assess it and coach if it goes wrong.

The more we use our phase of play and the more we coach drills using the coaching points the more experience and knowledge we gain.

This ironically means that we can let our players play more and only stop them when we see problems or need to correct errors. We do not now have to coach each point rigidly to everyone in a logical order. We are now much more flexible and able to coach our better or more experienced players.

This also means that we can improve our coaching within the popular small sided game format. We can let the game flow, allowing our players to learn through the game complimented by our observations, questions and answers with minimal interjections, coaching points and demonstrations.

So looking back at this phase of play what else can we use it to coach?

How about defending?

CHAPTER 7

Defending

If we look at the phase of play and the attacking team we can see that they have spread the ball wide to the left hand side.

What do we want to see from our defenders?

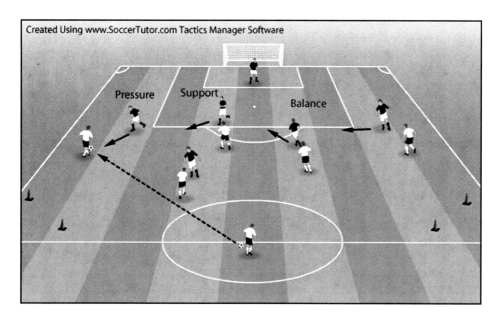

If we look at the diagram above we can see how our nearest defenders shuffle across to pressure and defend against the player with the ball.

This means the second defender has come across to support them and the third and fourth defenders again shuffle across to add balance to the back four.

This is all good movement and of course we would ask our players to tackle and try to win the ball.

When should our defenders tackle and when should they try to hold up the player with the ball?

How far should they move across?

Where should they be standing in relation to the ball and the attacker they are marking?

DEFENDING - SMALL SIDED GAME

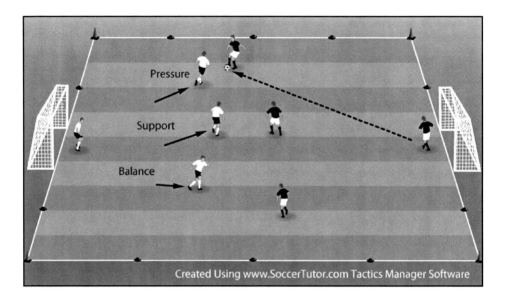

Created Using www.SoccerTutor.com Tactics Manager Software

Let's try to answer some of these question in our 4 v 4 small sided game, this time with goalkeepers in each of the two full-sized goals at each end of a 40x30 playing area.

The goalkeeper starts with the ball and passes the ball out to one of their three teammates. This team is now attacking and the other team need to work on defending the play and trying to win back the ball.

For younger players you may need to coach one team (as discussed before). If this is the case, it will change our free flowing small sided game into more of a drill.

If we do this we will work with the white-shirted team as shown, and their defending. The change we need to adopt is that we, as the coach, always start the game by serving the ball into one of the black-shirted players from the sideline to begin each phase of play in the drill.

As we know, in both the small sided game and the drill the coaching points remain the same.

So what are they?

Looking at the diagram and the fact that the ball has just been played from the goalkeeper to the wide right attacker, what would we, as the coach do now?

What is our first defending coaching point?

The first coaching point is the decision that is made by the nearest defender. The defender needs to decide if they can sprint to get to the ball first.

Can they intercept the ball as it is played from one opposition player to the other?

If the player cannot get the ball then they need to make the right decision, stopping in the right position to add pressure to the opposition player with the ball.

So, to aid our thinking process and progress through the coaching points let's imagine our defender did not nick the ball. Instead they are holding position and adding pressure to the player with the ball.

What do we need to get right next?

The three key elements are: the pressure on the player with the ball, the support from the next nearest defender and the balance of the next nearest players.

As we have just discussed, our closest defender is adding pressure to the attacker on the ball whilst our second nearest player has moved across to try and support the pressuring defender. The first and second defenders' job is to cut out, or at least close down the passing options of the player with the ball. The third nearest player should add balance to the defence and cover any more distant options.

The supporting and balancing defenders should occupy positions in between attacking players. In these positions the supporting player is able to cover the pressuring player or switch across to pressure their nearest attacker.

Likewise, with the balancing player they can switch between either moving forward to the nearest attacker, or moving away to the furthest from the ball.

What will we look at next?

Let's think about our defenders body shape. The defending players should adopt an open body shape so they can see both the attacker with the ball and any open attackers and their passing options.

Another time to think!

Let's think about our defenders.. What would we say their position should be in relation to the striker?

The defender needs an open body shape to see the attacker with the ball and any other attacking players. As is always the case, the defender of course needs to be goal-side.

What can we say to our defenders to make sure they can always see the ball?

"Goal-side and Ball-side"

The defender needs to be nearer to their own goal than the attacker but also slightly to the side nearest the ball. Our defenders cannot get into a position where the attacker blocks their view of the player with the ball.

Let's see how our defenders react to the position of the ball in a game.

Our defenders our goal-side and ball-side of the attackers.

Created Using www.SoccerTutor.Com
Tactics Manager Software

Is there any other reason why our defenders need to be goal-side and ball-side?

If the defender allows the attacker to get in front of them, or ball-side, they can show for a ball played across the front of their body and toward the goal. The defender cannot see through the attacker, allowing them to turn onto the pass and shoot.

Take another look at the diagrams and the position of the defenders relative to the attacker with the ball.

Seeing this in the diagram is the first step to seeing it in a drill or game.

The ball-side position of the defender has a second plus. It aids the next coaching point which is communication. If they cannot see everything they cannot give constructive instructions to the defender in front of them.

The defenders should use short sharp instructions that they all understand in order to keep team shape and compactness. For example we can use "pressure", "hold" or "drop off" as instructions.

What do we mean by these commands?

Pressure is obvious as we want the nearest defender to put pressure on the player with the ball. But "hold" and "Push" might be a little more confusing. For "hold" we mean holding a position across the pitch or to "Push" up the pitch and "hold" a higher line.

In this drill however, we should concentrate on the communication between

the nearest two defenders.

Can the supporting defender make the pressuring defender aware of their position and where they want the attackers to be pushed? A simple shout of "Inside!" Can accomplish this.

Can the pressuring defender show the attacker inside and into the supporting defender to make a 2 v 1?

Before we get carried away with team defending, let's take time out to step back and think about the very basics. Can we use this drill to simply coach 1 v 1 defending?

No, we simply need a 1 v 1 drill where we can concentrate on coaching the simple points needed to defend in a logical manner.

MOVE, RECEIVE THEN 1 v 1 DEFENDING - DRILL

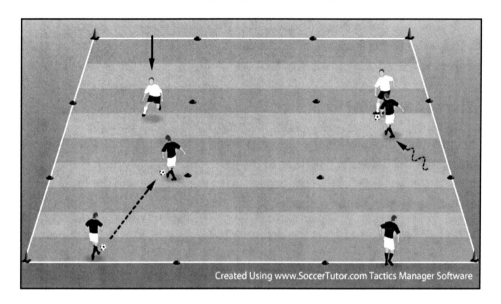

Created Using www.SoccerTutor.com Tactics Manager Software

Here we use the same format as in our 1 v 1 dribbling drill, three players, one at each end and one in the middle. The players should all rotate positions after a number of attempts so they all get the opportunity to defend.

To start the drill the player at the bottom passes the ball into the middle player who moves to receive the ball and attempts to dribble it over the end-zone ahead of them.

The first job of the defender is moving to close down the player with the ball. To this end, they should move when the ball is kicked. If the defender can get to the ball before the attacker then they should try to do so, remember can they nick it?

Let's think about the decision of the defender again.

What if they cannot nick the ball?

Our defender needs to stop and block the attacker's path adding pressure to

them as they try to dribble forward with the ball.

It may sound silly, but how would we want our defender to stand?

Firstly, can they get In line with the ball as they close down the attacker? Then, as they stop to hold up the attacker, can they do it half-turned; facing at 45 degrees to the attacker instead of face on.

Why at an angle?

Taking a 45 degree stance, the defender could actually influence the attacker's direction. If the defender half turns to the right it may actually push the attacker to the defenders right as that way opens up to the attacker and the route to the left is closed down by the defender.

Being half turned also allows the defender to be close in, ideally touch tight.

No closer as they will not be able to see the ball.

Why is this important?

The defender should always react to the movement of the ball and not the movement of the player.

If the defender cannot see the ball there is a danger they will react to the twists and turns used by the attacker to get away and fool the defender.

The defender should also be on their toes, enabling them to turn and sprint back should the attacker try to go around them.

To aid the defender we also need to look at their body shape.

Can they have their knees bent so they are always balanced and ready to make a move to tackle or turn and sprint?

The defender's head should also be steady and concentrating on the ball.

Now our defender is standing half-turned with the attacker moving towards them. The defender is balanced and concentrating on the ball, looking for any slip or mistake from the striker.

What next?

Our defenders need to be patient. The defenders should never commit themselves to a tackle they cannot win. The defender should not dive in, make a sliding tackle or go to ground. Once the defender is on the ground they are out of the game. They need to make sure that when they make the challenge they can win the ball. Therefore our defenders should be patient; concentrating on the ball to see if the attacker loses control and a tackle can be made.

Can they do more?

The defender should be positive and force the attacker to think.

Can they make a move or feint to tackle?

The defenders need to try and unbalance the attacker or force them to do something they do not want to do.

This has the added advantage of keeping the attackers focus on controlling the ball and not the game environment around them.

So what happens if the attacker loses control of the ball?

Time to tackle the attacker and win possession of the ball.

The defender will first need to decide which foot to tackle with.

Do we have any thoughts?

Speed is the key to winning the ball, so our defender needs to make their tackle with the nearest foot to the ball.

If both the attacker and defender are running in the same direction the defender may need to use the foot nearest the player to try and pinch the ball.

If the attacker is running at them, which direction do they try and go around them?

If the attacker goes to the defenders right then the defender needs to try and use their right foot to block the ball.

Remember sliding tackles, although fun, are a last resort and should be coached as such.

Let's think about adding some fun.

Any ideas to create a fun challenge for our players?

Which defender stops the most attacks?

Can they win possession of the ball and then run the ball over the attacker's end line for double points?

Can we progress the drill again?

Can we move from one attacker and one defender onto two attackers and two defenders.

Will this make a difference to our coaching points?

MOVE, RECEIVE THEN 2 v 2 DEFENDING - DRILL

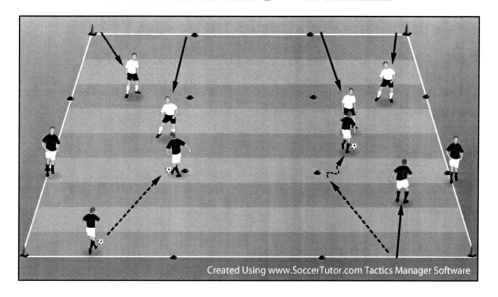

Created Using www.SoccerTutor.com Tactics Manager Software

To introduce 2 v 2 defending we simply move to three attacking players; one at each side, five yards infield and one in the middle of the end line with the ball. Two defenders start, one at each top corner of the opposite end line.

To start the drill, the player at the bottom passes the ball into one of the two attackers positioned five yards in and moves forward to create a 2 v 2. This is shown on the right hand side of the diagram, where the left side player and the central player attack the end line.

For our younger players you may want to start with an easier two defenders against one single attacker. In this case, just like the left hand side of the diagram above, the middle player passes the ball to one of the infield attackers (right sided player) and they attack the end zone on their own.

What do we think?

Remember, the first job of the defender is moving to close down the player with the ball. The defenders should move when the ball is kicked to see if they can nick it.

Let's think about the two defenders should they both simply follow the same coaching points as before?

No, only the first defender should follow the key factors for the single defender that we have discussed before. However, the second is the supporting defender and therefore needs to adopt a slightly different approach.

Firstly, we need to look at the positioning of the second defender.

The second defender should be behind the first defender and at an angle across towards the second attacker or the open side of the pitch.

How near?

The second defender needs to be no more than ten yards, ideally two or three from the first.

What about Communication?

The second defender is in a great position to observe the game and the attacking options. They should shout precise information and encouragement to the first defender. Can they influence the first defender by calling for them to "go tight", "wait", or "patience"? Can they show "inside" or "outside"?

What happens if the attacker gets past the first defender?

In this case, we need to reverse the roles of our defenders. If the first defender is beaten they must recover behind and become the support to the second defender who moves forward to pressure the attacker.

Let's speed it all up and have a bit of fun.

We still need to concentrate on defending and the coaching points involved but can we apply them in a more relaxed environment?

DEFENDING - CIRCLE DRILL

Here we have our players positioned in a circle, but this time we start with two defenders in the centre of the circle and the ball at the feet of a player on the outside circle.

The player on the circle with the ball starts the drill by passing it across the circle to another player on the circle. These players on the circle then try to keep passing the ball around the circle.

Simply put, the two defenders need to work together to try and win the ball.

How?

They need to use the same coaching points we have just discussed.

- Decision – Can the defender get to the ball and nick it?
- Pressure – Which defender is closest to the ball and therefore able to apply pressure to the player with the ball?

- Support – Which defender is supporting and what position will they adopt in relation to the ball and the pressuring defender?

- Body Shape – Can the defender adopt a half-turned body shape, 45 degrees to the player with the ball? They also need to be on their toes, knees bent and their weight slightly forward ready to challenge.

- Patience – The defenders should not dive in and commit themselves to a tackle they cannot win. Don't go to ground.

- Concentration – Watch the ball and react to its movement, not the movement of the player.

- Positive – Can the pressuring defender affect the attacker by feinting to tackle or move in a certain way, trying to force the attacker in the opposite direction?

- Technique – Tackling quickly with the nearest foot as soon as the opportunity arises, but only when they know they will win the ball.

- Communication – The supporting defender needs to offer support and instructions to the pressuring defender.

- Recovery – If the pressuring defender is no longer nearest to the ball the roles of the two defenders needs to change and fast.

So what is the challenge?

Which pair of defenders limit the attackers on the circle to the least number of consecutive passes?

Keep score and challenge the next pair to beat the current record.

Keep changing the players in the middle to give everyone a chance to defend.

With younger players or players of differing skills we might want to add a challenge rather than a scoring system. In this case we could reward the defender making the ball winning tackle by swapping them with the attacking player who loses the ball.

Let's move on again and try and introduce more of a game related 2 v 2 challenge.

DEFENDING 2 v 2 - FUNCTIONAL DRILL

Created Using www.SoccerTutor.com Tactics Manager Software

Here we have a line of defenders positioned behind the goal where the six yard box intercepts the byline. Strikers are positioned on the other six yard, byline intersection. The coach stands just on the edge of the centre circle with a number of balls ready to start the drill.

On the coach's command to start: two defenders, black shirted in the diagram above, and two attackers, white shirted, race out from the byline. The attackers are allowed to run directly towards the coach to collect a pass. The defenders, however, have to run around cones positioned on the edge of the penalty area before being able to engage the attackers.

The positions of these cones are dependent upon the speed and skill of the players involved, the better the players the wider the cones are placed.

The functional drill is now a simple 2 v 2 scenario with the attackers trying to work a shooting opportunity to score past the goalkeeper positioned in the full-size goal. The two defenders need to work together to stop them.

What do we coach?

Obviously we need to coach the same defending coaching points. However, some are a little more important in this drill.

What do we think affects the whole drill?

The speed of the attackers and defenders as they race out to receive the ball, or defend, is paramount. If the defenders do not react quickly enough then the attackers will be given a free run in on goal. The defenders need to get to the receiving player and add pressure as soon as possible and therefore as high up the pitch as possible.

Are there any other changes?

There is a change in communication between our players. Our goalkeeper is now in a good position to see the complete game situation so they are now perfectly placed to shout encouragement and instructions to the defenders.

What else do we think about this drill?

This is a defensive drill that counteracts all we talked about in our playing through the middle chapter of this book.

So with this in mind do you think we could use the functional drills and phase of plays in that attacking chapter to actually coach defending?

Could we use this drill to coach 2 v 2 attacking?

Yes, simply change the coaching points and the players you coach.

So what happened after we played the ball through the middle?

Chapter 6 went on to discuss our attackers playing out wide and attacking down the wings. So will this affect our defenders and our current coaching points?

Can we use a functional drill from our playing wide chapter to coach defending?

DEFENDING CROSSES - FUNCTIONAL DRILL

In the defending crosses version of the playing wide functional practice we again use the five attackers playing against two defenders within the centre circle. We can also use the same three passes rule before they pass the ball to one of the wingers. The winger must then dribble or run with the ball beyond the end cone before crossing the ball.

Again, we can have the two central attackers starting on the "D" of the penalty area alongside the two central defenders ready to defend the cross.

Firstly, do we remember what the advantage is of using a functional practice in training?

We continually recreate the same scenario that we want to coach our players and try to improve. Here, we continually create crosses from both the right and left for our defenders and goalkeeper to defend.

What did we give the strikers as coaching points?

- Mental Strength – Commitment and determination.
- Movement – Fast and direct.
- Shooting Technique – One touch finish: Accuracy and power.
- Control – If they need to control the ball, can they do it so they get a shot off with their second touch?

So having said this to the strikers what do we think we need to tell our defenders?

The first two points are just as relevant to the defenders as the attackers.

- Mental Strength – Commitment and determination to get to the ball first and clear it. They should use whatever method they can; this could be their head, feet or simply just getting in the way.
- Movement – Fast and direct straight at the ball to get in front of the attackers and clear it as quickly and effectively as they can.
- Obviously we will need to change the second two points.
- Shooting Technique needs to change to clearance.
- The defenders should stay deep until the ball is crossed and watch the flight of the ball and close down the attackers as the ball travels. The defensive clearances should have height and distance.
- Control needs to change to control and communication.
- The goalkeeper needs to take control of the situation and communicate to their defenders what they want. The goalkeeper's communication needs to be clear, concise and calm. They need to instruct their defenders by shouting instructions dependant on the cross. Typical clear instructions are "Keeper's" if they can catch it, which will alert the defenders to move out of the way. The goalkeeper could shout "Away" if they want the defender's to deal with the cross and clear it or "Safe" if the cross is going out of play.

Can we progress this again, is there another defending situation?

We have dealt with defending through the middle and from wide areas in the attacking third of the pitch but what about defending in the middle third of the pitch and possibly against more players?

DEFENDING OVERLOADS - FUNCTIONAL DRILL

Created Using www.SoccerTutor.com Tactics Manager Software

In this functional drill we use a coned area 40x30 or 50x30 dependent upon the skill, strength and the ability of the players. We use a wider rather than longer area as the midfield area is usually a wider zone to defend in a game and so for the purposes of this drill we spread our defenders or midfielders across it. To this end, we use the 30-yard lines as the end zones.

The seven attackers (black-shirted team) play against the five defenders (white-shirted team) within the coned area. The team that gets the ball across the opposite end line scores a goal. A throw in can be used to restart play should the ball go out of the coned playing area.

To begin coaching our players how to defend against an overload, the attackers will have to be told to play keep-ball. The first attacker begins the drill by playing a direct ball across the area to another attacker deep on the opposite side, as shown.

Our white-shirted defensive team needs to start in a 3-2 formation, with three defenders pushing to pressure, support and balance while the two further defenders support them from behind.

How and what do we need to coach when defending against an overload?

The defending coaching points are the same again but we will need to tweak them and elaborate on them to fit the situation in the drill and what we need to coach.

Let's look again at our first coaching point the defenders decision. Can the defender "nick it" and intercept the ball when the pass is played between the attackers? Our defenders should move when the attackers head goes down. This is the "Trigger" for them to move into position or sprint to intercept.

What about the defensive formation?

The pressure, support and balance of our nearest defenders are paramount. Again, the closest defender should add pressure to the attacker with the ball pushing them infield, compacting the play and closing down the space. The defence should always try and maintain their shape, drifting forward rather than sprinting as the attackers could play around them.

The other defenders offer support and balance by moving into triangle formations just behind the attackers, these are shown in the diagram above. These triangular "goal-side and ball-side" positions enable the defenders to see the ball and the attackers and therefore the attacking options.

From the diagram above, can we see what other advantages these triangular positions afford our defenders?

This position allows our defenders the best opportunity to intercept a pass. More importantly, it allows our defender to switch roles quickly, moving straight from the supporting or balancing role into the pressure defender with the others switching and falling in line behind them.

The last defender is also vital, staying deep to prevent the long pass, out ball

option, and hence adding more pressure by cutting down this attacking option. This last defender can also see the full area and is therefore in a great position to communicate hold, push or drop.

Let's look at what we have coached the attackers in the same situation and reverse it to try and understand both situations.

What would we say to the attackers?

Spread the play, create gaps in the defence and try and play through and around them.

So, for our defence we want the opposite: compactness. The defence needs to stop the attackers going forward by reducing the space of the play, forcing the attack infield and into the other defenders. By making the play compact and applying the pressure the attackers are forced to play negative balls, this will hopefully force them into making mistakes.

Any attacker on the opposite side of the coned area to the ball should be thought of as no direct threat at that present time and ignored by the pressing defenders. The deep defender should drop out and watch the whole game play area though, preventing the long lofted pass which would alleviate the compactness and pressure on the attackers. The defence should remember if the nearest defender to the ball pressures the attacker then the team should pressure the attackers, "one go and they all go".

Why?

The defenders have to work together. If one player goes tight and adds pressure on their own then the attackers could play around them. Therefore if one defender goes to add pressure and close down the space all the defenders should move together as a unit.

What happens if one player goes to pressure and gets beat?

The defender needs to recover into another defensive position. Hopefully our defender has listened to some of what the coach has said and not dived in, ending up on the floor. Instead they are still on their feet and able to turn and

sprint back in behind the nearest defender or back possibly at the attacker to make a further challenge. This is our defenders recovery run.

We can also make recovery runs across the pitch, not when a player is beaten but when the ball is switched directly from one side of the pitch to the other by the attacking team. Just as we tried to coach the attackers during our switching play drills.

If the attackers manage to switch the play from one side to the other then the "rope effect" should take effect. This is where each defender sprints across to the side the ball is whilst keeping the same distance between them. This way our defenders try to keep compact by simply moving as a block across the pitch compacting the play nearest the ball.

Is there anything else we might want to add about our defenders positions?

Remember our defending small sided game where we spoke about positions, pressure, support and balance?

What about stressing the importance of being both goal-side and ball-side to our defenders again?

Let's try and put all this together and coach our defensive unit in a more game-related environment.

Let's look back at the phase of play diagram we saw right at the start of this chapter. We had the attacking team play the ball right out wide to the left hand side to spread the play.

What do we want from our defenders?

DEFENDING 6 v 6 - PHASE OF PLAY

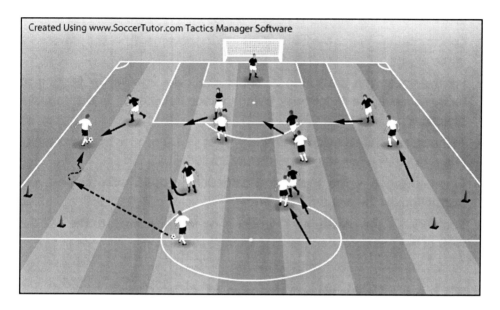

Here we see our half pitch again and the two target goals wide out on either side of the half way line. The attacking team is trying to score past the goalkeeper in the full size goal and the defenders are trying to win possession and play the ball into a target goal. We can start the phase of play with a free pass played by the deepest attacking midfielder from on, or just beyond the half way line.

So what do we want to see?

We want to see our players thinking about all the coaching points they have been told and using them to stop the attackers.

So what do they need to do?

- Decision – Can the defender get to the ball and nick it?
- Pressure – Which defender is closest to the ball and therefore able to apply pressure to the player with the ball?
- Support – Which defender is supporting and what position will they adopt in

relation to the ball and the pressuring defender?

- Body Shape – Can the defender adopt a half-turned body shape, 45 degrees to the player with the ball? They also need to be on their toes, knees bent and their weight slightly forward ready to challenge.

- Patience – The defenders should not dive in and commit themselves to a tackle they cannot win. Don't go to ground.

- Concentration – Watch the ball and react to its movement, not the movement of the player.

- Positive – Can the pressuring defender affect the attacker by feinting to tackle or move in a certain way, trying to force the attacker in the opposite direction?

- Technique – Tackling quickly with the nearest foot as soon as the opportunity arises, but only when they know they will win the ball.

- Communication – The supporting defender needs to offer support and instructions to the pressuring defender.

- Recovery – If the pressuring defender is no longer nearest to the ball the roles of the two defenders needs to change and fast.

Let's have a think about the aim of defending?

Is it to stop the attackers?

Yes, but there is so much more we want for our better players and teams. They need to tackle the attackers, break up play and win possession of the ball. We then want to convert defense into attack and quickly.

Have we anything in this phase of play that helps this?

Yes, the target goals on the half way line give our defensive players the chance to win the ball and look to go forward. Even better, our players are looking to go out wide which would naturally take them out of the way of any attacking players around them.

This is great for our younger players as it gets them looking up and moving into the right areas when they win the ball, but what about our better players?

Can we make the phase of play more game realistic?

Let's remove the target goals and replace them with a defensive team player on the half-way line. This player can move all the way across the half-way line but not back into their defensive half. This player should watch the play and the position of the ball and move in relation to it offering as a passing option to any defensive player who wins the ball.

So what are the advantages of having this new player?

It is now not just a simple matter of moving out wide, knowing where they need to go or move to get to the fixed target goals. Now our defenders need to win the ball and look up immediately, very often whilst still under pressure, and see where the pass forward is.

Is this new player learning through the phase of play?

Do we remember the strikers moving across the line drills?

In that small-sided game just like now we want our strikers moving across the pitch to show for a pass. This is another opportunity to take a set of coaching points and using it in a different drill where again the same scenario can be introduced to help the play.

We should always try to remember the drills and coaching points and then analyze the drill or phase that we are about to coach. Is there a cross over or a chance to merge two scenarios and create a new drill which helps us and more importantly more of our players?

Can we just take a minute to concentrate on this important transition and the quick change from defense to attack.

How can we create this quick transition environment and more importantly repeat it for our players to experience over and over and therefore learn from it.

COUNTER ATTACKING - SMALL SIDED GAME

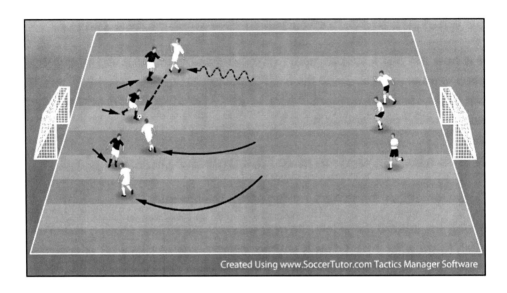

Created Using www.SoccerTutor.com Tactics Manager Software

Here we have a small sided pitch suitable in size to the age and ability of our players. In our small sided game we have a 3 v 3 v 3 game but you could use a 4 v 4 v 4 if you had more players. There are two target goals at each end, but you could just as easily allow the players to run over the end line to score.

Our drill starts with the ball at the feet of one of our players in the central area, in this case the team all in white. The black-shirted team lines up to the left hand side goal and the team in black shorts line up toward the right hand side.

The central team, all in white, then attacks the team to the left and try to score in the target goal, in what is essentially a 3 v 3 game. If they score a goal is awarded and they take the position of the black-shirted team and stand ready to defend the left sided goal.

If the central team shoot and miss or the defending team wins possession of the ball, then they immediately attack the team to the right. As their attack ends the central attacking team once again moves passively aside, taking the position of the black-shirted team that was defending the left hand goal.

The diagram above shows the transition stage as the all white team attacking the goal to the left lose possession of the ball to the defending black-shirted team.

In the diagram below we see the black shirted team counter attacking at pace, attacking the white-shirted team and goal to the right. As we can see, the all white team have simply moved aside and across to defend the goal to the left.

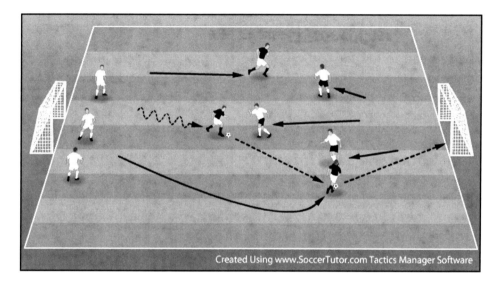

Again, the same rules of the small 3 v 3 game apply. The black-shirted team attack the team to the right trying to score in the target goal. If they score again we award a goal and they take the position of the white shirted team and stand ready to defend the right sided goal.

If the black shirted team shoot and miss or the defending team wins possession of the ball, then they immediately attack the team to the left, now the all white team. As their attack ends the black-shirted team once again moves passively aside taking the position of the team defending the right hand goal.

This drill can now simply revolve through the teams and players attacking each goal in turn.

So what can we say about the moment the defending team wins the ball?

Our players need to turn defence into attack, moving from compact to expansive as quickly as possible. Let's think about the passing options we want in our fast paced counter attack.

Where do we want our supporting players in relation to the player winning possession of the ball?

Have we got time to play the ball across or backwards to supporting teammates?

No, we need to get forward quickly so our passing options should ideally be ahead of the ball. The transition from defending to attacking triggers the movement of our supporting and balancing defenders as they sprint forward to offer passing options ahead of the ball.

What about the pass forward?

If possible, the player in possession needs to pass the ball ahead of the receiving player so they can run onto the ball without breaking their stride pattern and therefore keep the momentum of the move going.

Before we continue our journey let's just take a minute to recap.

We have looked at 1 v 1 defending through 2 v 2 and onto 3 v 3 and then into a small sided game. We then moved onto functional drills and looked at defending crosses and then defending against an overload.

Working on the 6 v 6 game, we discussed the transition from defence to attack and onto the counter attack. These are all the tools we need to combat the attacking drills, small-sided games and phases of play we talked about in the previous chapters.

So what is the next logical progression?

What do we ultimately want to be able to understand and coach?

Let's move onto coach defending in a 7 v 7 game.

DEFENDING 7 v 7 - MINI-SOCCER GAME

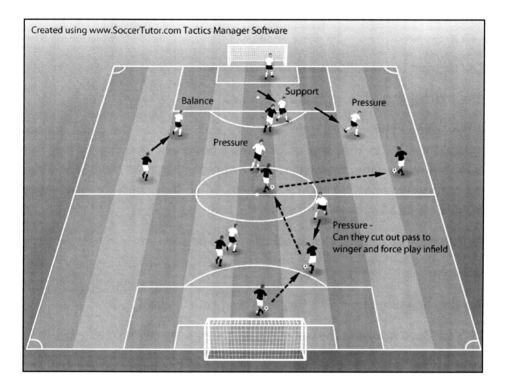

Here we see our players set out as two 7 a-side teams on a standard mini-soccer pitch.

Now can we use everything we have learnt to coach defending in this game?

Firstly, we should remember with our younger or less experienced players to only coach one team, in this case we will concentrate on the white-shirted team.

So let's look at the diagram above and go through each of the players as they come into play.

The ball starts with the black-shirted goalkeeper and is played to the central defender.

What do we think is the first thing we need to look for and coach?

The nearest attacker should make a decision dependent upon the speed of the throw or pass from the goalkeeper.

Can they nick it?

Can they get to the ball first and win possession?

The attacker should move as the ball moves.

If the attacker cannot nick it they need to look up to see the game options around them before they stop quickly by the opponent receiving the ball. This is so they can position themselves to pressure the player on the ball and also cut out any easy passing options for them. When they reach the player they need to create a big barrier and watch the ball.

As the coach we need to look at our defenders position and body shape.

Is it right?

Are they half-turned and effecting the player with the ball?

Let's continue following the ball as it is passed into the central midfielder.

Here we see our defensive midfielder pressuring the player on the ball and trying to push them wide to their right.

Why might they position themselves to do this?

Communication, the central defender has told them to push the play that way.

Observation, the player has seen that the left winger is free and not marked so they try and cut out this pass, pushing the play in the opposite direction.

We, as the coach, need to ask ourselves questions as we watch and listen to what is unfolding. We cannot just coach the players robotically barking out the coaching points in a logical order. We need to evaluate why our players do things and work out who, if anyone, is actually at fault and why.

We will move on again following the ball in the diagram as the attacking

midfielder plays the ball out wide to their right sided midfielder.

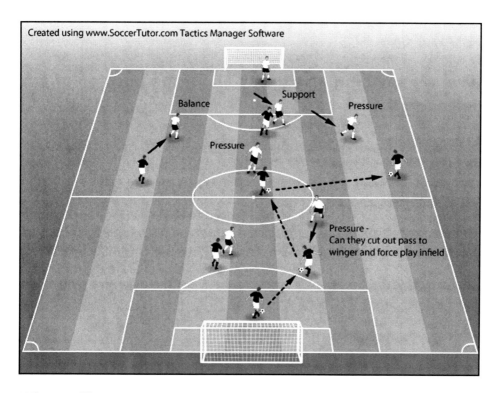

Created using www.SoccerTutor.com Tactics Manager Software

Balance

Support

Pressure

Pressure

Pressure -
Can they cut out pass to
winger and force play infield

What will we say to our left sided defender?

- Move as the ball moves – Get into line with the ball if the pass is slow can they nick it. If they cannot nick it, can they move at the same pace as the pass, keeping square to the ball at all times.

- Body shape – When reaching the player the defender needs to put up a big barrier and settle into a 45° defending stance.

- Concentration – Watch the ball and react to its movement, not the movement of the player.

- Patience – The defender cannot dive in, they need to wait for the opportunity to tackle the opponent.

What about the rest of the defenders?

Support and balance. The support and balance of the team is very important.

If the left sided defender moves over to cover an attacking right winger, as in

the diagram, the right sided defender should move across to a more central position to help balance the team. The midfielder should also move across and back to add cover.

Have we anything else to say about the position of our defenders?

All our defending players should be both goal-side and ball-side. This is so they can see the player they are marking and the player with the ball. More importantly they can see the passing options and are in a great position to actually intercept any pass.

We have spoken about the compactness across the pitch but what about up the pitch?

What would you think about a large gap between the defensive midfielders and the defenders, ?

Is this an area the attackers might use?

I am sure we have all heard about the attackers that drop off to use the gap between the midfielders and defenders, receiving the ball half-turned and ready to begin an attack. With this in mind we need to coach our players, making sure our defensive midfielder drops to cover this critical space

We have coached defending in our 7 v 7 game but can we move into 9 v 9 and what are the differences?

DEFENDING 9 v 9 - MINI-SOCCER GAME

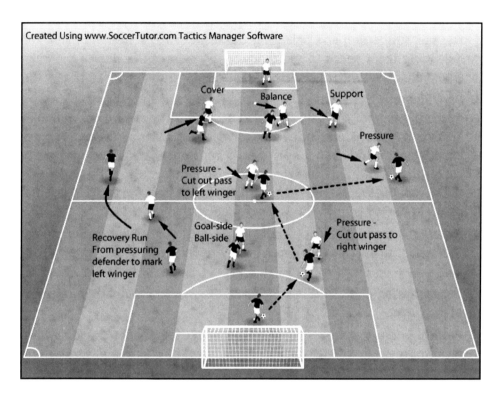

Created Using www.SoccerTutor.com Tactics Manager Software

Here we see our players set out as two 9 a-side teams. Remember that with our younger or less experienced players we should only coach one team; in this case we will concentrate on coaching defending to our white-shirted team.

Let's take the opportunity to look at the diagram above and see if we can assess the players, their movement, their positioning and if they have done everything we have talked about and coached.

Once again, to do this we need to know and understand the coaching points for defending.

1. **Decision** – Can the first defender (in this case the defending team's striker) get to the ball and nick it?

2. **Pressure** – Which defensive player is closest to the ball and therefore able to

apply pressure to the attacker that has the ball? This will first be the defending team's strikers again then the midfielder as the ball moves forward.

3. *Support* – Which defender is supporting and what position will they adopt in relation to the ball and the pressuring defender? Should they pressure or hang back? What is the nearest defender doing?

4. *Balance* – The defending team needs to be compact, with players pressuring the ball, supporting and balancing the team shape across the pitch. The defending team needs to move across to compact the side of the pitch where the player with the ball is.

5. *Body Shape* – Can the defenders adopt a half turned body shape, 45 degrees to the player with the ball. They also need to be on their toes, with their knees bent and weight slightly forward ready to challenge. Defenders must, in addition, try and cut out open passes into danger areas. The first pass to cut out in this diagram is into the attacking right sided player. This is done by the striker. The second pass to cut out is the pass from the attacking central player to the left winger. This is the defending midfielder's job.

6. *Patience* – None of the defending players should dive in and commit themselves to a tackle they cannot win. The defenders should stay on their feet.

7. *Concentration* – Watch the ball and react to its movement, not the movement of the player.

8. *Positive* – Can the pressuring defender affect the attacker by feinting to tackle or move in a certain way trying to force the attacker in the direction they want them to move?

9. *Technique* – Tackle quickly with the nearest foot as soon as the opportunity arises, but only when they know they will win the ball or it is the last chance to block a cross or shot.

10. *Communication* – The supporting defender needs to offer support and instructions to the pressuring defender. The goalkeeper also needs to communicate and tell the defenders about the whole game situation.

11. *Team Shape* – The defending team needs to be compact across and also up and down the pitch. As the coach we need to look at the distances between the strikers and midfielders, the midfielders and defenders and then the defenders and goalkeeper as any gap can be exploited by the attacking team.

There is one thing we have forgotten in our list and something that is critical to coaching defending in a game scenario.

Can we look at the diagram and see what we have missed?

We need to remember to coach the recovery runs. If the pressuring defender is beaten or no longer nearest to the ball then the roles of the defenders needs to change and fast. Any recovery run should be made to get back to the nearest attacker, toward the centre of the goal or toward the nearest goal post in the case of the wide players.

With younger or less experienced players we need to coach one team, one theme, but what might we want to do with our better players and more importantly be able to do as better coaches?

Our better players might easily cope with instructions aimed at both teams.

But it will need more than an experienced coach with detailed knowledge of all the coaching points. It will need one who can oversee the whole game environment with the understanding of both teams play.

In this advanced environment we may even have two experienced coaches working together. They could take a team each and even coach them different things. One coach might be coaching the attacking and one the defending.

Can this be done on the same drill?

Yes of course, but both coaches need to understand each other and allow each other to stop the game to explain points. Of course we cannot keep stopping the game, so only stop the game for "urgent issues" otherwise save up some advice and comments and when a natural stoppage occurs step into coach.

So let's see how much we have learnt and now understand as coaches.

Let's take a look at our 9 v 9 game and look at the phases of play one by one in order to test ourselves and what we might see and coach.

What might we think about the ball being played into the central midfielder by our attacking team?

What drill have we looked at in this chapter that fits this phase of play and what we want to coach?

The defending 1 v 1 on page 195 is perfect.

Created Using www.SoccerTutor.com Tactics Manager Software

This details the position of the defender in relation to the player receiving the ball. It also lists and explains the specific coaching points as they wait for the opportunity to win the ball.

Is there anything else we want to add?

Let's add the defending small sided game on page 190 as this helps our nearest player but also the supporting and balancing players we see in the 9 v 9 game.

What have we just done?

We have taken our theme of defending and produced a session.

We have begun with a technical 1 v 1 defending drill where we coach the finer details of trying to win possession of the ball. Then we move onto a small-sided game and look at the way the players need to interact and help each other as a team to defend.

What drill can we progress onto to complete our defending session?

Let's use the current 9 v 9 defending game where all our players are involved

and practicing their defending skills.

Now let's turn it all on its head and test our understanding further.

The challenge now is to coach the attacking team and specifically within the same phase of play where the ball is being passed into the central midfielder.

What drills will you use?

Let's think what we need.

Moving to receive the ball and receiving skills.

We could use the strikers' movement squad drill on page 41. This is where we have our player moving to create space for the pass before receiving the ball half-turned ready to play forward.

So we can use this drill to coach these points, but does it really fit with what we see in the 9 v 9 game?

No, we need to add an opposing player or players to further challenge the player.

Can you progress onto another drill?

How about the receiving and shooting drill on page 45. Here we have a logical progression into a 2 v 2 challenge in the central area.

Where next though?

In our 9 v 9 game it looks like they are playing the ball wide to attack down the wings, so what does this allow us to progress onto?

Let's use the crossing small sided game on page 107.

Why this one?

It incorporates the pass into a forward player and then the rule that a goal can only be scored from a cross which promotes the lay-off out wide.

Another question.

We are on the training ground now and although the game is going well and

the players are generating lots of crosses and shooting opportunities, they are not converting them into goals.

What will we do?

Can we change a session half way through to take into account what we are seeing.

Of course, if we have the knowledge and experience we can quickly call a drinks break and set up something new. It needs to be very quick and easy to set up and something that will help our players.

Can we think of anything?

Let's think about the knowledge we have gained through this book, is there anything we can use.

Headers and volleys on page 116 is easy to set up, fun, challenging and importantly offers repetitive crossing and shooting opportunities.

How can we finish the session?

Simple, use this same 9 v 9 game but this time instead of coaching defending and its coaching points, we can adapt it and use it for coaching attacking and shooting.

Let's take the whole process one stage further before we finish. Here is a diagram showing how players offer support in a game.

CHAPTER 8

Match Analysis

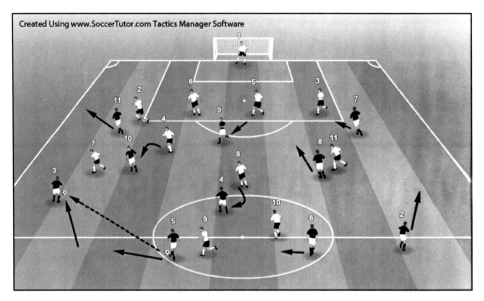

Created Using www.SoccerTutor.com Tactics Manager Software

Let's look at the 11 v 11 game diagram above and analyse what we see.

The ball has been played from the centre back into the left sided defender and this has triggered the movement of all the other players to support and offer passing options.

Time to work backwards, all the way through the book we have modified and changed the drills creating logical progressions to allow us to coach and improve our players. The challenge now is to analyse the movements and tactics we see on the pitch, or don't see from our players, to create drills and small sided games that we can use to coach our teams.

So what is the first thing we see as the left sided defender receives the pass?

What do their team mates do?

What is happening in the area nearest the ball?

What can we see in the diagram?

Can we create a format to coach what we see?

Let's look a bit more closely at the left sided defender with the ball and the nearest three players.

Here is the diagram again, but this time to help us analyse the play we have highlighted the first area of concern.

Can we think of any kind of drill or game that seems to fit with what we see?

The highlighted area contains eight players, four from each team so this fits exactly with the 4 v 4 small sided games we have previously developed and used.

But what are we going to coach?

What do we see from the players in possession of the ball?

Movement to create space for a pass.

Passing options ahead, to the side and behind the ball.

PASSING OPTIONS - SMALL SIDED GAME

Created Using www.SoccerTutor.com Tactics Manager Software

So let's use a 4 v 4 small sided game to coach this movement and support. Here we have a 40x40 playing area split into thirds, the two end thirds or "safe zones" are much thinner than the central area, we can use 5x40 for each end zone. At each end of the area we have a small target goal.

The teams start with 3 v 3 in the larger central area and a single player in each of their own safe zones.

The game begins with the ball at the feet of a player in one of the "safe zones" The other players cannot enter the end zone until the player with the ball dribbles forward or passes the ball into the central area, starting the game. Once the game starts all our players are allowed to move into any of the zones.

Why might we need the player starting the drill to be able to dribble into the central zone?

Let's think about the 3 v 3 we have in our central third and our younger or less experienced players.

It is more difficult for our players to get free to receive a pass when the opponents are marking our players man to man in the 3 v 3 area.

Allowing our fourth player to dribble into the central area means they can dribble toward an opponent and engage them, which allows another of our players to move away from them and into space.

Now the game is started what are we going to coach?

What do we want to see from the team in possession of the ball?

Movement to create space for a pass, ahead, to the side and behind the player in possession of the ball.

Now as the coach we need to draw on our technical knowledge of the situation and what we want to coach our players.

What specifically will we coach?

- Create space – The receiving player's movement to create the angles and distance for the pass.
- Know where the defender is – The attacking players need to know where the defenders are.
- Awareness - The attacking players need to be on their toes and anticipate a pass at any time.
- Decision – The player should make their decision of which type of receiving skill to use based on the defenders position, run onto the ball at pace or receive half turned.
- Technique – Did the player receive the ball correctly using the appropriate long barrier or half turn technique?
- End product - The player should have the ball under control and be able to play the next pass, dribble, run with the ball or shoot.

Now we need to look back at the main 11 v 11 game diagram and make some more coaching points relative to that environment, the players and the tactics of the team.

Let's think about the player on the ball.

Can we think of anything we might want to add?

- Create space – Does the player with the ball engage a defender to create space for others?
- Know where the defender is – The attacking players need to know where the defenders are in relation to their team mates, who is in space and in a position to receive the ball?
- Awareness - The attacking player needs to be aware of what is going on around them and when they should release the ball.
- Decision – The timing and direction of the pass, did it go to the best player and quickly enough?
- Technique – Did the player pass the ball correctly, weight, speed and direction.
- End product - After a good pass to a team mate do they stop or move into a supporting position?

Have we missed anything?

Tactics, team shape, supporting players and their passing options.

During the small sided game we should continually look for our four players to offer passing options for the player on the ball.

Do our players continuously move to create passing options ahead, to the side and behind the man with the ball.

Do our players pass and move?

Do they support and show for the next pass?

These are the things we should be analysing and coaching are players, can we keep them passing and moving to create space to receive a pass.

Let's go back to the main 11 v 11 diagram again and see if we can use it to highlight another coaching drill. Can we progress this small sided game as well and find something a little more demanding and game related?

Here is the 11 v 11 game diagram again, but this time we have increased the highlighted area.

Created Using www.SoccerTutor.com Tactics Manager Software

What do we think about the highlighted area now?

How does it fit with what we have learnt already and does it compliment any drill format, small sided game or phase of play?

The highlighted area contains twelve players, six from each team so adding a couple of goalkeepers would make a 7 a-side mini soccer game which we could use.

But what are we going to coach and what format will we use?

We need to progress the small sided game we have just looked at and the passing and movement to create space to receive a pass. We have more players to watch and coach but we need to keep the game environment. We could use the 7 a-side game format but maybe a phase of play would be better used to coach the same tactics and skills as in the small sided game.

So let's use half a pitch with a couple of target goals placed at the half way line and a full size goal at the other and set up our phase of play.

PASSING OPTIONS - PHASE OF PLAY

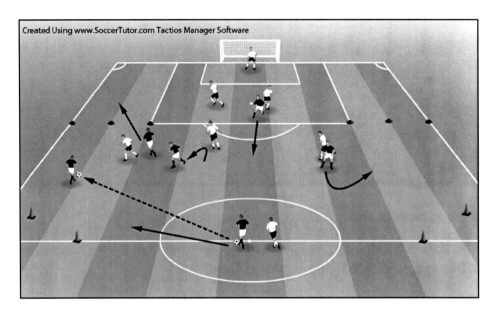

Created Using www.SoccerTutor.com Tactios Manager Software

Here we see our half pitch again and the two target goals wide out on either side of the half way line. The attacking team is trying to score past the goalkeeper in the full size goal and the defenders are trying to win possession and play the ball into a target goal. We can start the phase of play with a free pass played by the deepest attacking midfielder from on, or just beyond the half way line.

There is something different from our normal phase of pay. We have added a line of marker cones all the way across the pitch in line with the edge of the penalty area and a opposing player is standing next to the deep attacking midfielder who starts the drill with the ball.

Do we have any thoughts?

What did we need to make sure happened in the small sided game for our less experienced players?

Again, we need to make sure we have a passing option into the midfield to start the drill.

As the coach we need to think about the drill and how can we do this?

We need to make sure we have an overload, in this case a 4 v 3 in midfield. This is a forced overload created by three simple instructions.

1. The attacking team must start the drill with a lone striker positioned beyond the line of cones along the edge of the penalty area.

2. The defending team must start the drill with two defenders positioned beyond the same line of cones, this creates a 2 v 1 in that final third.

3. The defending team must have a midfielder positioned next to the deep attacking midfielder who starts the phase of play. This defending player cannot join the phase of play until the ball is passed into midfield.

Once the phase of play starts all the players are unrestricted and can move wherever they like.

So again we ask, what specifically will we coach?

All the coaching points we discussed before, along with the team tactics, team shape, supporting players and their passing options.

During the phase of plays we need to continually look for our nearest three players. Are they moving away from their defenders to create passing options ahead, to the side and behind the player on the ball.

But what about the other players?

Do we want our striker to drop into the gap between the defenders and the defensive midfielders and if so do they do it?

If we do want them to drop deep, do we want another attacking midfielder to swap roles and go ahead of them to show for an attacking pass?

By using this phase of play we can discuss our tactics and practice these movements with our players. We need it to become natural for our players to make these movements in a game and understand where they should support in relation to the player with the ball.

Let's get back to our 11 v 11 again and look for the next progression.

Looking at the 11 v 11 game diagram again we have highlighted another area.

Created Using www.SoccerTutor.com Tactics Manager Software

What do we think about this new highlighted section of the game?

Space, tactics and game awareness.

Can we use this area?

In the game we continually see our wide defender in possession of the ball look for a forward pass down the line or just inside, to the nearer midfielder.

It looks like our players are aware of this highlighted space, as in this case, the right sided defender has pulled out further to the right to take advantage of it. But our players do not get the ball across to them.

So our analysis of the game shows our players are struggling to pass the ball across the pitch to switch the play.

What shall we do?

Can we look at the 11 v 11 diagram and our players to try and come up with a drill, phase of play or game where we can coach this skill?

11 v 11 SWITCHING PLAY - FUNCTIONAL DRILL

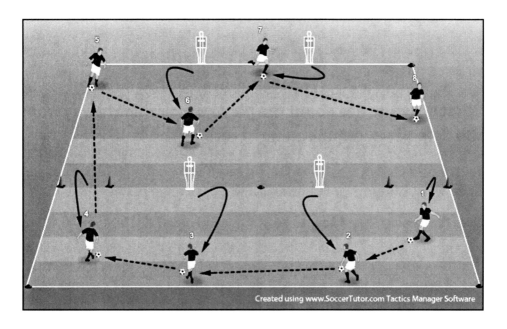

Let's take our four defenders and four midfielders and set them out across the pitch as in the 11 v 11 game diagram.

This functional drill can now be used to recreate the passing sequence we want.

Here we see our players switch the ball across the back four players, forward, and back across our midfield.

But what do we coach?

Can we remember the functional drill we used previously?

What were the coaching points?

- The players need to move off the defender quickly to provide a passing option.
- They also need to look at receiving the ball facing forward allowing them to switch the ball quickly across the pitch.

- We also need to look at the pass: are they played to the safe side?
- What about our players technique, can they receive and pass in two touches or even turn their body as the ball comes across them to pass across with one touch?

Is there anything different from the previous drill?

Is there anything we have modified to better suit our players and the game environment?

What do we notice about the players movement away from the defenders, mannequins to receive the ball?

The midfield players, numbered five, six, seven and eight drop backwards and sideways away from their defensive mannequins to offer passing options.

Does the passing always have to go in numerical order?

Can we miss out a player?

Yes, of course. Just like in a game, if the opportunity is on we can miss out a player to play a longer or more direct pass across the field.

We need our players to take responsibility, be technically sound, creative and strong enough to make decisions.

How though?

We need to think about the drills we use, how and why we use them.

We need to analyse what we see, what are players do, how and why they do it.

We need to give them the environment that allows them to develop, understand but also challenge themselves and be adventurous.

We need to support and provide our players with everything they need to become as good as they can be and I really hope this book helps you in providing that environment.

SUMMARY

We started with one of the most common drills in widespread use today, our simple shooting drill. We then spoke about the most common coach we see using this drill. The one we see commentating on each and every player's shot without one single useful word or action to correct them.

This was the basis and starting point for our coaching journey which began with a look at why this is not a drill or coaching style we should promote.

We continued through a variety of functional drills and small-sided games on various themes and looked at how to use them to coach our teams. We concentrated on coaching points and the specific details which we need to know and understand in order to coach effectively.

Phases of play were introduced followed by 7 v 7 games and we looked at the specifics of using these and how they can be broken down into bite size portions for the inexperienced coach.

Hopefully this journey has given us more confidence and understanding of how we can use these coaching points to coach within functional drills, small-sided games, phases of play and games.

This journey and the way it has progressed will hopefully help us the coach's coach. Building our knowledge through detailed coaching points to help us understand and analyze drills, sessions and actual passages of play in a game.

I do not in any way present this book as the single answer to successful coaching, but I do offer it in hope that it will aid coach education as we all try to improve and in doing so improve our players.

Lightning Source UK Ltd.
Milton Keynes UK
UKOW031937090712

195714UK00006B/29/P

9 780956 675255